Oxford Modern Britain   SERIES EDITOR: JOHN SCOTT

Kinship and Friendship in Modern Britain

The *Oxford Modern Britain* series comprises authoritative introductory books on all aspects of the social structure of modern Britain. Lively and accessible, the books will be the first point of reference for anyone interested in the state of contemporary Britain. They will be invaluable to those taking courses in the social sciences.

Oxford Modern Britain

Kinship and Friendship in Modern Britain

Graham Allan

OXFORD UNIVERSITY PRESS
1996

Oxford University Press, Walton Street, Oxford OX2 6DP

Oxford New York
Athens Auckland Bangkok Bombay
Calcutta Cape Town Dar es Salaam Delhi
Florence Hong Kong Istanbul Karachi
Kuala Lumpur Madras Madrid Melbourne
Mexico City Nairobi Paris Singapore
Taipei Tokyo Toronto
and associated companies in
Berlin Ibadan

Oxford is a trade mark of Oxford University Press

Published in the United States
by Oxford University Press Inc., New York

British Library Cataloguing-in-Publication Data
Data available

Library of Congress Cataloging in Publication Data
Allan, Graham A.
    Kinship and friendship in modern Britain / Graham Allan.
        p.   cm. — (Oxford Modern Britain)
        Includes bibliographical references and index.
        1. Family—Great Britain.   2. Kinship—Great Britain.
    3. Friendship—Great Britain.   I. Title.   II. Series.
    HQ614.A57   1996   306.85'0941—dc20   95–50916
ISBN 0-19-878124-5
ISBN 0-19-878125-3 (pbk).

1 3 5 7 9 10 8 6 4 2

Typeset by Best-set Typesetter Ltd., Hong Kong
Printed in Great Britain
on acid-free paper by Biddles Ltd, Guildford & King's Lynn

For Kahla,
who knows more than most about the complexities of kinship

Foreword

The Oxford Modern Britain series is designed to fill a major gap in the available sociological sources on the contemporary world. Each book will provide a comprehensive and authoritative overview of major issues for students at all levels. They are written by acknowledged experts in their fields, and should be standard sources for many years to come.

Each book focuses on contemporary Britain, but the relevant historical background is always included, and a comparative context is provided. No society can be studied in isolation from other societies and the globalized context of the contemporary world, but a detailed understanding of a particular society can both broaden and deepen sociological understanding. These books will be exemplars of empirical study and theoretical understanding.

Books in the series are intended to present information and ideas in a lively and accessible way. They will meet a real need for source books in a wide range of specialized courses, in 'Modern Britain' and 'Comparative Sociology' courses, and in integrated introductory courses. They have been written with the newcomer and general reader in mind, and they meet the genuine need in the informed public for accurate and up-to-date discussion and sources.

John Scott
Series Editor

Acknowledgements

Many people contributed to the writing of this book directly and indirectly. I would like to thank Graham Crow in particular, who has always been a ready source of support and assistance with his extensive knowledge of wide areas of sociological writing. I am also grateful to my other colleagues in the Department of Sociology and Social Policy at the University of Southampton. Despite all the pressures on university departments at the moment, it remains an excellent place in which to work. I would especially like to thank Doreen Davies, Glynis Evans, Gwen Gordon, and Eileen Upward for the support they have shown me over the years. Parts of this book were written while I was visiting the University of North Carolina at Greensboro and the University of Maine at Orono. My thanks to Rebecca Adams and Bob Milardo for arranging these visits and making me welcome. Although Sue Allan and Lynn Watson were not directly involved in the writing of this text, it wouldn't have been written when it was without the very different support they have given me when it was needed.

Contents

List of Activities, Tables, and Figures

Chapter One

Introduction

Sociology and the study of informal relationships

At times it seems that sociology is essentially concerned with the structure of social relations at a level which explicitly ignores the individual. The view that society is more than the sum of its parts is taken to its extreme, so that the personal relationships with which every individual is involved are seen as sociologically somewhat peripheral — interesting at an everyday level but of little sociological consequence. Often indeed informal relationships — or personal relationships as they are often known — are seen as essentially the province of psychology, especially social psychology, rather than sociology. Yet this view is mistaken. The study of personal relationships is as fully a part of our understanding of the social world we occupy as the analysis of industrialization or property relations. Thus, issues of solidarity, cohesion, and conflict — what it is that binds people together or creates divisions between them — cannot be understood properly without recognizing the importance of the informal, personal ties which individuals develop and sustain. Informal relationships represent only one aspect of this, but they are an important one. It is through these personal bonds that people develop attachments and form commitments, come to appreciate their place within the social order, and co-operate with one another in generating change.

With a little reflection, it is evident that informal ties play a significant part in many areas of social life. For example, in looking at socialization, it is evident that both family and peer group are major influences on the ways in which children, and indeed adults in later life, come to define themselves as social beings and develop an image of their self. Studies of educational achievement also point to the influences of these relationships and, in particular, to the ways in which the articulation of values between home and school can be crucial in affecting a child's response to the schooling process. Studies of deviance also emphasize the ways in which informal relationships of different types influence the individual's actions. Whether the perspective taken is, for example, a subcultural or a labelling one, group membership and informal association are seen as significant in the creation of deviant identities and behaviour. So too, from the famous Hawthorne experiments in the 1930s onwards, studies of the workplace have recognized that informal solidarities between co-workers play a part in shaping their responses to a range of workplace issues. Similarly, in studies of local communities it is inappropriate to focus exclusively on formal organizations. What also needs to be considered are the sets of personal ties which bind people together, how people use these to achieve their different ends, and how these relationships impinge on more formal aspects of community structure.

Many more examples from different areas within sociology could be given here. You may choose to think of others for yourself and reflect on how the informal relationships of different sorts which people sustain affect their behaviour in those spheres. The general point to recognize is that in many areas of social activity, informal relationships actually play a major part in shaping people's attitudes and behaviour and giving meaning to their lives. These relationships matter. They matter at a personal level, but they also matter more widely in terms of social organization. Within contemporary society, formal organizations and bureaucracies have, without doubt, become increasingly significant. Yet while the character and tempo of modern social life is governed by their operation — think how much of our lives are ruled by the timetables which bureaucracies of different sorts set — in many respects, it is the informal relationships we have which make all this possible. For as well as providing us with a sense of self and individuality, the various informal relationships which we are involved in also enable us to navigate our way around the demands and contingencies of everyday living. Far from being social 'luxuries' of little sociological consequence, these ties are, to use Jerrome's analogy, 'the cement which binds together the bricks of social structure' (1984: 715).

The study of informal ties is thus too important to leave solely to psychology. While psychologists have every right to be concerned with personal relationships — and the development of the 'new psychology of personal relationships' over the last fifteen years is particularly welcome in its emphasis on relationships rather than individual personality (Duck, 1990) — sociology too, with its different questions, concerns, and frameworks, also has much to offer the analysis of informal ties. That is, as well as the study of these ties being quite central to some of the key issues within the discipline, a sociological approach also makes a major contribution to our understanding of the way these relationships are socially constructed and organized.

Kinship and friendship

This book does not aim to deal fully with all these issues. Its remit is rather more modest. Its aim is to explore kin and friend relationships from a sociological angle. Other informal relationships could, of course, have been chosen for inclusion in the book, for example, those between neighbours or between colleagues and workmates. There are two main reasons for limiting the discussion to kinship and friendship. The first of these is simply the constraints of space. To have included a wider range of informal ties would have meant curtailing the examination of kin and friend ties quite significantly. While this is possible, it would have resulted in the analysis being much shallower. In the case of kinship in particular, it was judged better to provide a fuller account of these relationships so that their patterning could be appreciated and understood. The second reason for concentrating on these particular types of informal relationship is that they carry more weight than other informal relationships. Typically people invest more in them, and expect more of them. They play a larger part in people's consciousness, provide them with a fuller sense of social participation, and contribute more to their image of self than do other categories of informal relationship.

However, neither friendship nor kinship has been studied very extensively by sociologists, in line with the relative unimportance attached to personal relationships generally within the discipline. Unlike some other areas of sociological investigation, there is relatively little written on either of these topics. Friendship, in particular, is something of a Cinderella topic within sociology, in Britain but also elsewhere. The last ten years has seen a growth in interest, with more books and scholarly articles being published (see, for example, Allan, 1989; Jerrome, 1992; O'Connor, 1992), but the basis of our knowledge is still slim. Many of the ideas and much of the data about friendship emanates from the United States. Whether the results of studies in the US can be straightforwardly applied to Britain is a difficult matter. Certainly we need to be cautious of assuming that what is the case in one society is also the case in another.

The situation with regard to kinship studies in Britain is certainly better. The 1960s in particular was a period when our understanding of contemporary British kinship developed significantly. Unfortunately, after this period interest in the topic waned, so that since the early 1970s there have been relatively few studies which focus explicitly on kinship (Wilson and Pahl, 1988). A good number of studies make some passing reference to kinship issues, but rarely has this been the main topic of analysis. It is only in the late 1980s and early 1990s that there has been a resurgence of interest in Britain in the sociological analysis of kin behaviour, partly as a consequence of the inadequacy of contemporary political assumptions about the character of kinship responsibility in providing care for those who are in need of support (see Finch, 1989).

While the book is focused primarily on kinship and friendship, in the process it hopes to foster a broader understanding of the significance of informal relationships in social life. That is, as well as examining patterns of kinship and friendship, it also seeks to illustrate that a sociological approach to the study of informal relationships is both valid and informative. In doing this, it will review our current knowledge of kin and friend ties, examine how they are patterned, and analyse their role within the social realm. It will look at how these different relationships are organized; at the variation there is in this; and at whether these ties are socially, as well as personally, important. More broadly, it will be concerned with the role of informal solidarity in contemporary society.

The organization of the book

The main focus of the book is on kinship and friendship. However, before examining these relationships in detail, it is worth considering some of the dominant claims about the impact of contemporary social conditions on informal relationships generally. This will provide a framework for better understanding the character of friend and kin ties in modern Britain. This is the subject matter of Chapter 2. In particular, the chapter will examine ideas about the privatization of social life and the decline of communal relations, ideas which are common both in popular discourse and in academic debate.

The following four chapters then concentrate on kinship ties. Chapter 3 is a scene-setting one which discusses some of the complexities of kinship and introduces some of the major kinship studies which have been undertaken in Britain. Chapter 4 continues with this theme, but focuses predominantly on the issue of whether Britain can be said to have a kinship system in operation. The focus of the chapter is largely on secondary kin relationships, that is ties with aunts, uncles, grandparents, and cousins. Chapter 5 is explicitly concerned with the character of primary kinship. It examines the ways in which parent-child relationships are patterned over the life-course, and also discusses the significance of sibling ties in people's lives. Chapter 6 analyses how kinship obligation is generated and whether kinship behaviour is negotiated rather than normatively prescribed. In doing so, it focuses particularly on old age, infirmity, and care-giving.

Chapters 7 and 8 examine patterns of friendship. In Chapter 7 the nature of friendship ties will be discussed, along with class and gender variations in the ways they are constructed. The chapter is also concerned with change in friendship patterns and the consequences of material and social inequalities between those who are friends. Chapter 8 develops some of these themes in examining social aspects of friendship. It concentrates on two particular issues. The first part examines how the opportunities people have for friendship are patterned by their social situation, while the second part is concerned with the social benefits of friendship — the ways in which friends support one another and the contribution friendship makes within the wider social order.

The final chapter, Chapter 9, returns to some of the issues raised in Chapter 2 about the impact of modernity on informal relationships, especially with respect to the theme of the privatization of social life. In doing this it focuses on the extent to which a social-network perspective can help generate a fuller understanding of the significance of informal relationships in contemporary society. It argues that while such an approach has limitations, it nonetheless offers a framework for investigating informal relationships which has advantages over more traditional approaches.

Chapter Two

Social Integration and Social Change

Various theories have been developed to explain the changes that have occurred in kinship and other personal relationships in recent times. Most, though not all of these, take their starting-point as the process of industrialization, though sometimes this is specified as the growth of urbanization or the development of a capitalist economy. As well as having different roots, the theories differ in the details of the processes which have affected the patterning of personal relationships. Yet, in the main, these different theories all tend to paint a broadly similar picture, even those which are explicitly concerned with developments in the late twentieth century (Giddens, 1992). This picture is one which sees the decline of more communal and extensive solidarities and an increased significance placed on individualism and the construction of the private sphere.

Classic examples of such perspectives are the theories of community decline which have become part of the heritage of popular thought. Beginning with the work of Tönnies (1955), but since taken up by many other sociological thinkers, the argument is that before the industrializing process took hold, people lived in relatively small communities, and consequently knew others in those communities well. People relied on one another for their needs, and were thus highly interdependent. This itself generated high levels of informal control, with everyone being privy to a great deal of knowledge about one another. Even when people were geographically mobile — which they were more often than is commonly assumed — the same principles soon applied to the personal relationships they developed in the new localities in which they settled. The social control exercised over them was greater because of the high level of integration of those within the locality who controlled employment, religion, and justice. Thus community life is seen as having been integrative and to some extent oppressive in its controls. There was relatively little tolerance of individual freedom.

Industrialization is held to have changed all this. The extensive interdependencies and consequent solidarities were broken by the growth of factory production and the economies of scale this allowed. People no longer were part of small-scale societies but instead lived in urban areas with large numbers of others with whom they had few personal ties. The local area might have been an important reference for them, but the patterns of formal and, importantly, informal control which previously existed no longer held their power. Individuals were freer from supervision, freer to construct lives outside the gaze of others. In the process, it was held, moral values altered. The commitment to the collective, the sense of being a member of a larger whole, disappeared as individualism took a firmer grasp. In such ways, the importance of the local, of community ties based around a shared physical location, waned. No longer did people feel a sense of community belonging or a community commitment in the way they had under the previous socioeconomic system.

Now, this type of argument has taken many guises. Historically two have been particularly significant within the sociological study of personal relationships. The first of these arose with the Chicago School of sociology in the 1920s and 1930s. Its main premisses and theoretical concerns were brilliantly expressed by Louis Wirth in his paper 'Urbanism as a way of life', first published in 1938 but since reprinted extensively. In this paper Wirth argued that it was urbanism rather than industrialization which generated change in people's life-styles, including the patterning of their informal relations. Urban culture, common to all urban areas, was generated by the size, scale, and heterogeneity of cities. Instead of people being united by common bonds and a common heritage as was the case in rural areas, urban locations brought together people who not only had little in common but who also had little to tie them to one another. In the city, interdependencies were lessened and those that existed were impersonal. In his famous phrase, social contacts in the city became 'impersonal, superficial, transitory and segmental' (1938: 12). Each individual relied on few others but was surrounded by many. The need for formal controls became paramount — the clock and the traffic light symbolized this as much as anything. According to this view, under the new conditions of urbanism, informal ties became of less social significance in their power of control and coercion, almost a social luxury of little consequence.

The second main theme developing from ideas about the loss of community focused more specifically on what had been happening to the family. Here the argument tended to be that with industrialization and the dominance of individual wage-labour, the dependencies that held the family together no longer applied. In particular, as families no longer depended on common property for their well-being, as it was claimed they had, for example, in family farming, each individual was freer to further her or his own economic interests independently of those of other family members. There was little to tie adult generations together, and little need for siblings to co-operate. As a result, it was argued, the nuclear family came to replace the extended family as the dominant form of household as industrialization gathered pace. Increasingly the nuclear family became 'structurally isolated', in Parsons' (1956) famous, though frequently misunderstood, expression (Harris, 1969; Allan, 1985). That is, members of the nuclear family were no longer dependent on other kin, though at least some of these other kin remained central in their lives. While the historical basis of these claims has rightly been questioned (see, for example, Anderson, 1971), they were certainly influential in sociology in their time and captured themes which were current in popular thought.

Now a good deal of empirical research in sociology has sought to demonstrate that these rather grand overviews of the changes occurring in informal relations misrepresented social reality. A great deal of effort was exerted, generally successfully, to show that not all informal ties were 'impersonal, superficial, transitory and segmental' (not that Wirth actually claimed that all were), that communities existed in urban areas, and that kin wider than the nuclear family continued to be important. Indeed some of the most famous studies in British and American sociology focused on these issues (see, for example, Young and Willmott, 1957; Gans, 1962; Pahl, 1965; Rosser and Harris, 1965). Yet in many ways, these authors appeared to be fighting a losing battle. Certainly informal relationships can be shown to be important to people — the other chapters in this book demonstrate that — and it is wrong to view informal relationships as just personal ties — they are also significant at a social-structural level. Nonetheless, and precisely because they are structurally and not just personally significant, it would be strange if they were not influenced by the changes in social and economic organization which have been occurring since the early industrializing period. The perspectives outlined above may not capture these changes perfectly, but if nothing else it is difficult to make out a strong case that membership of integrated social collectivities based upon locality or family has become a more powerful influence than in the past.

Rather than discussing these general issues in greater depth, this chapter will focus on one particular branch of these ideas: the privatization thesis. This thesis has attracted a good deal of attention in sociology, especially in Britain since the publication of *The Affluent Worker* studies (Goldthorpe *et al.*, 1969). As with ideas about the breakdown of contemporary communities, the principal argument is that with modernity the character of people's social participation has altered. In general, life has become less public than it once was; people are better able to protect their privacy from the gaze of others. The segmentation of different activities, the separation of home from employment, and the changing position of family and the domestic sphere in people's consciousness have led to a major change in their patterns of social involvement and the significance of informal relationships in their lives. It is this which makes ideas about privatization useful in the context of the present volume. It allows a framework for exploring the changes that have occurred in kinship, friendship, and other informal ties, even if in the end the thesis is judged unacceptable or incomplete.

However, evaluating ideas about privatization is no more straightforward than evaluating the other perspectives mentioned above (Procter, 1990). In particular, there is no single argument advanced about either the causes or the consequences of the increasing degree of privatization which is posited. Rather, as a general perspective, the thesis entails a number of related strands, with different authors emphasizing some above others. In order to assess the extent to which social participation has become more privatized, it is useful to keep some of these different strands analytically separate. This will allow for the development of a better appreciation of the role of family, friends, and other informal relationships in modern Britain and other advanced industrial societies. In the rest of this chapter, then, some of the main arguments made in support of the privatization thesis will be summarized so as to provide a framework for interpreting the personal and social significance of informal relationships in contemporary social life.

Components of privatization

At the centre of the privatization thesis is the notion that the private realm of family, home, and domestic relations has increasingly become detached from the public sphere of employment, organizational activity, and participation in public arenas of sociability. Moreover, it is the private sphere, rather than the public one, to which the majority of people are most committed. Whereas once there was a feeling of public, communal solidarity, this has disappeared and its place has been taken by a far more fragmented, individualized attachment to the personal realm of family and home. Clearly linked to the 'breakdown of community' thesis, claims for the privatization of the modern world nonetheless emphasize the replacement, rather than the disappearance, of older loyalties by new forms of solidarity, though frequently there is a sense of regret that civic participation is being undermined. The vision is of an atomistic society in which individual households and families get on with their lives with little reference or concern for anything other than their familial welfare and private interests.

Thus there are two sides to these claims. The first concerns the increased prominence given to family matters; the second the lesser involvement of people in activities outside the domestic realm. Importantly, these are seen as operating both at the level of activities and of consciousness. In other words, it is not just that people are spending more time and devoting more energy to family relationships; it is also that they want to. They consider this legitimate; it is seen as a satisfying and rewarding project giving meaning to their lives. Indeed there is often a sense of regret, verging sometimes on a lack of fulfilment, if, for whatever reason, such family experiences do not materialize. In order to examine the role of informal relationships in contemporary life and evaluate the idea of the modern world becoming privatized, these two themes — the centrality of the domestic-familial complex in people's lives and the decline in significance of external social participation — will be considered separately.

The domestic sphere

So has the family and domestic sphere become more central in people's lives over time? This is a much harder question to answer than it appears, in part because the form of the question is too general. In particular, one needs to question whether the changes mooted have affected everyone equally, and whether all have experienced them in the same way. However, before doing this, we can examine the types of argument forwarded in support of privatization about family change. One set of arguments concerns the greater weight given to nuclear family relationships. As we saw above, the argument that nuclear family ties take precedence over more extended ties has been a common theme within the sociology of the family. Certainly, as the chapters which follow will discuss, people's greatest commitments and obligations are to primary kin, especially partners and dependent children. Over time it appears that these commitments have become greater, for some at least. Let us consider first the developments occurring in the way marriage and equivalent partnerships are constructed, then look at the place of childhood in social life, and finally in this section look at the place of the home in people's consciousness.

Marriage

Strong claims have been made that the character of marriage and other couple partnerships is altering, with heightened expectations of the personal satisfactions that these intimate relationships can provide. These ideas have long been present in popular and academic writing on the family. Early formulations emphasized the shift from marriage as an institution to marriage as a companionship. More recently there has been an emphasis on conjugality, on 'sharing', and on mutual fulfilment. In Cancian's (1987) phrase, 'marital blueprints' — what individuals hope for, expect, and work towards in their marriages — have altered to reflect a greater focus on the couple relationship as a source of personal fulfilment rather than social, economic, or sexual convenience. The change in language in recent years from that of marriage — wife, husband, spouse — to that of 'partner' is indicative of these emergent shifts, in which the emphasis is increasingly placed on the relationship as a personal construction in which social convention plays a reduced part. Indeed, the marriage act itself has largely been reconstructed from a social and legal act of contract to a symbol of personal commitment.

Of course, it is important here not to confuse the reality of marriage with ideological dreams. Often marriage fails to live up to the 'blueprints' the couple desire. Certainly it is easy to demonstrate, as many studies have (Oakley, 1974; Edgell, 1980; Mansfield and Collard, 1987; Morris, 1990), that marriage continues to be an unequal 'partnership'. The domestic division of labour may not be as marked as it once was, but it is a highly gendered division in most marriages. Just as the employment structure continues to discriminate against women in the opportunities available, so too the tasks of child care and housework remain defined predominantly as female ones. Current high levels of divorce also highlight the discrepancy between ideology and reality in marriage, as does the prevalence of marital violence. With almost half of marriages ending in separation, it is evident that many couples are not successfully achieving their goals. However, the increased divorce rate rather supports the arguments that the vision people have of marriage is being transformed. In other words, it is largely because their marriages as constructed relationships are not providing them with the level of personal fulfilment and satisfaction they desire that people are terminating them.

Thus notwithstanding the inherent problems of meeting contemporary expectations, there can be little doubt that many couples seek to find a higher level of intrinsic happiness in their marriage, rather than simply accepting its extrinsic benefits. The creation of the personal relationship increasingly becomes its own end; it is seen as a means of authenticating the individual and of expressing and defining the self. Studies like Mansfield and Collard's (1987) demonstrate the power of this ideology in people's choices to marry. So too the common idea that marriages need 'working at' indicates the extent to which marriage is seen as a personal project capable of providing the individual with meaning and self-realization. The increasing use of counsellors and other relationship 'experts', together with the prevalence of articles in popular magazines dealing with relational dilemmas, also attest to the growing significance of these relationships in our contemporary world-views. Giddens, in his book *The Transformation of Intimacy* (1992), has developed such arguments furthest, pointing to the emerging connotations of intimacy and commitment in couple relationships in late modernity. From this perspective, the present age certainly appears to demonstrate a fascination for reflexivity about intimate relationships which appears to have been largely absent in previous eras. This emphasis on the centrality of intimate relationships in our lives, on intimacy as a project, is consonant with the thesis that the personal and the private are now privileged over the public and communal.

Childhood

As with our views on marriage, so too our social beliefs about childhood have altered significantly over the course of the twentieth century. One obvious indication of this is the growth of schooling, which reflects the societal acceptance that children need special care, attention, and treatment if they are to prosper and develop satisfactorily. In addition to greater state expenditure on education and increased length of schooling, other services to cater for children's perceived needs have expanded and the absolute rights of parents have declined. The rise of health visiting and social work as professions owes much to our changing perceptions of children's requirements, as does the changing constitution of children's legal services. In Britain the Children Act of 1989 reflects the evolving concerns there are about the appropriate ordering of childhood experience. Equally the dominance of the cultural view, supported by the theories inherent in many psychotherapies, that experiences in early childhood influence, if not fully determine, people's personality and psychological well-being in adulthood is a very powerful reflection of the changed social construction of childhood in late modernity.

These social and cultural developments have obviously had an impact on families, a major site within this social construction of childhood. While it is now clear that more children than was once thought are abused both physically and sexually, and many more feel psychologically damaged by their upbringing, it is also apparent that children are the focus of much attention within families. At a very simple level, markets for children's goods and services have increased quite dramatically. Even allowing for higher living standards, the amount of money devoted to children's clothes, toys, leisure activities, books, and other 'educationally relevant' artefacts has mushroomed. Similarly, within many families, children are a major topic of conversation. Parents appear to worry at length about their children's development, monitoring and reflecting on their behaviour with a passion that would have made little sense earlier in the century. Similarly, it appears that children's voices are listened to within families much more than in the past. They may not have a right to 'vote' on key decisions, but they do seem to be routinely consulted and involved in many mundane family issues.

While these types of change have occurred, to differing extents among different groups, it is harder to judge whether they can be read as indicating a greater concern for children or just a different pattern of concern. It is certainly not possible to say that the experience of childhood is somehow 'better' or more 'fulfilling' than in the past, or indeed whether parents 'love' their children more. Like childhood, love itself is a social construction that really only makes sense within the socio-economic and cultural context within which it occurs. However, it would appear that children have become rather more of a focus of attention within families than was the case in earlier phases of modernity. Even here though caution is needed, as the argument applies far more clearly to fathers than to mothers. Children, especially young children, have long been a dominant focus of mothers' identities, shaping the pattern of their social participation in numerous ways. The detailed content of caring work may have changed in recent decades but its overall importance in the structure of many women's experiences has not altered so evidently.

The home

However, the argument about privatization does not rest solely on the changes there have been in the way that people seek to organize their domestic and intimate relationships. Another important element in it concerns the changes there have been in the way people have come to define the home as an arena of activity. There are a number of elements to these changes, but, as with the discussion of family relationships above, at their core is the way in which the private sphere has come to be insulated from the public sphere. As the prime physical (as well as symbolic) site of the private realm, the use of the home is likely to prove significant if privatization is occurring. Certainly there have been many changes in the conditions of the home over the course of this century, though the variations there are in people's experiences should not be ignored. It is for example a simple task to show that the material conditions of home life have improved quite dramatically even in the last fifty years as a result of technological innovation and economic change, fostered by a political desire to improve housing standards. Nonetheless there are very large inequalities within the housing market. Average housing conditions have risen, but there are still significant sections of the population living in unfit and inadequate housing. These differentials in housing standards certainly need to be borne in mind in the discussion that follows.

The more significant changes there have been to the home since the beginning of this century include the almost universal introduction of electricity and gas; a large decline in housing densities; better amenities, including the provision of inside lavatories, hot water, and fixed baths; the ready availability of domestic machinery; the introduction of centrally controlled heating systems; improvements in the quality and range of domestic fixtures and furnishings; extensive home leisure equipment; and rapid changes in housing tenure. It would be surprising if such radical changes as these had not led to any shifts in the ways people perceive and utilize the home. For the great majority of people, these changes have made the home a much more pleasant place to be. The developments in domestic life-style made possible by these changes should not be underestimated. All these changes have made the home a rather different experience for the majority of people.

Other changes occurring in the housing system have also influenced the ways in which the home is experienced. For example, the programmes to improve the housing stock after the Second World War led by the early 1960s both to the clearance of a number of slum areas in the major cities and the building of new estates on the urban periphery. This involved the decline of what are often seen as 'traditional working class areas' (see Crow and Allan, 1994), together with the close-knit social relationships which often developed in such localities, and the movement of people to new locations in which to begin with they were surrounded by strangers. Over time, informal ties developed between residents, but for many the experience of living in the new estates was quite different to their life-style in their previous homes. While the houses were attractive because of their higher standards, better amenities, and lower densities, at the same time there was a lower level of social participation and an absence of informal support (Mogey, 1956; Willmott and Young, 1960; Willmott, 1963; Crow and Allan, 1994). Many families were far more isolated than they had been previously. In some part, it was the experience of such families that helped fuel the idea of privatization as an emergent trend.

The growth in home ownership over the last fifty years has also contributed to a changed notion of 'home'. Increasingly 'a home of your own' has come not to mean simply one in which you live independently of your parents or other kin, but now more a home that you (and your partner) are buying (see Crow and Allan, 1990). Thus in the middle part of this century only a quarter of households owned (or were buying) their homes; the remaining three-quarters rented privately or from a local authority. By the 1990s this number had increased to two-thirds. There has been much debate in the sociological literature over the last decade about the significance of this change for people's understanding of the home. Some have argued that it has generated greater 'ontological security' — a greater sense of being in control of your own life (Saunders, 1990). Others have claimed otherwise, saying that local authority and housing association tenancy can also provide an equivalent sense of control (Forrest et al., 1990). Which view is right is not

---

Activity 2.1 Living in the Past

Imagine how different your life would be if you had no electricity in the home; you had to bathe either in a tin bath filled from the kettle or else in a public wash-house; the only toilet was outside; and you shared a cooker with two of your next-door neighbours.

Some of the more influential community studies of the 1950s and 1960s, including Young and Willmott's *Family and Kinship in East London* (1957), were undertaken in areas where such a lack of facilities was normal.

---

overly important here. The key issue is that the growth of home owner-ship within the society has certainly influenced the perception which people in general — be they owners or tenants — have about the place of the home in their lives.

There is one further change that is worth mentioning here. This concerns the growth there has been in the markets for home equipment, accoutrements, and furnishings. The development of these markets has had a major impact on the changing fabric of the home. Thus in comparison to, say, thirty years ago, not only has the range of home leisure equipment — hi-fis, televisions, videos, computers — grown enormously, but so too has the range of home furnishings and the possibilities for decoration. In addition, technological innovation has spawned an enormous do-it-yourself industry, as evidenced by the growth since the 1980s especially of specialist supermarket chains. Tasks which not that long ago were well outside the capabilities of most individuals are now quite routine (Pahl, 1984). Thus, overall, there is a much stronger sense of the home as a personal (or couple) creation. The home, it can be argued, has become much more a centre of self-expression than it was. Arguably, this sense of creation, of moulding the fabric of the home to reflect your tastes and style — however much borrowed from current fashion — is more important than the growth of owner-occupation in establishing the home as a place over which you exercise control. Of course, the extent to which this occurs depends on the resources available. As always there is a class division here, particularly between those who have household earnings and those who are dependent on state benefits and living in poverty. Nonetheless, this change in the ways it is now possible to shape and modify the ambience of the home represents a major cultural shift in people's understanding of what 'home' means.

Social participation

It is largely because of these changes in the domestic-familial sphere that the idea of privatization has taken such a firm root in social thought. But there is also a concurrent belief that people's social participation has become more privatized. That is, it is not just that the domestic-familial arena looms larger in people's consciousness but also that they are less concerned and less involved in sets of social relations outside the home. Whereas once people led more 'communal' lives, now they are much less involved in sociability with others. Their close family matters, but there is less commitment to social solidarity with a wider circle of others. It is these ideas with which this section of the chapter will be concerned.

To begin with, it is worth noting that the image of the past presented here can be questioned. Many sociable activities had a public dimension, occurring in pubs or the street, but equally people have long been concerned to protect their privacy and limit the knowledge other people have of their family's affairs (Pahl and Wallace, 1988). In many ways this was more important under the housing conditions of three or four generations ago than it is now. Increasingly with a reduction in housing densities and shared facilities, privacy can be assumed in ways in which previously it could not be.

Moreover, the extent to which social lives were lived in the public realm can easily be exaggerated, with the divisions between people being ignored (Devine, 1992). Thus men's social activities and relationships were relatively communal, frequently taking place in public arenas of one sort or another. Their work was often long and arduous and their active leisure frequently spent outside the home with their mates in pubs or clubs. (See Dennis *et al.*, 1956 for a classic account of this style of sociability.) Women's lives, though, tended to be rather more home-centred. There were opportunities for meeting others they knew in the neighbourhood while shopping or taking children to school. But there is little evidence of organized female sociability in public settings. These points are important, for not only do they highlight the variation there is in different people's sociable patterns, but they also lead us to question what privatized and non-privatized sociability actually is.

Consider first the variations that inevitably exist in the ways in which sociable activities are patterned, now or in previous eras. As later chapters in this book will argue more fully, sociability is not just a matter of personal choice. The patterns which emerge are also consequent on the social positions people occupy. As noted, gender is one factor here that has affected people's opportunities for different forms of sociable interaction. Class too is important in shaping the ways in which sociable ties are developed. The types of work people do, the demands it makes of them, the rewards it provides, the time constraints it imposes, are all likely to influence the ways in which sociability is organized (Wellman, 1985).

Equally, family circumstances will be important in structuring the opportunities and constraints there are for social participation. Thus people with young children have different opportunities than those who have adult children; single people are likely to develop different patterns from those in partnerships. What matters overall here is the constellation of commitments which individuals have, and of course the ways in which these change over an individual's life-course. Collectively these different commitments encourage the emergence of distinct patterns of sociable activity among different groups of the population (Allan, 1989). There is not one single pattern which can be taken as characterizing everyone's current experiences.

But it is also important here to question exactly what privatization implies about the character of informal solidarities with kin, friends, and neighbours (Allan and Crow, 1991). What is it that is being contrasted with the 'public' or 'communal' sociability that is supposed to have characterized previous times? Often the assumption seems to be that individuals and households are now far more isolated than they once were. Each person and each household is held only to be focusing inward, unconcerned about wider social involvement. Numerous studies have shown this portrayal to be wrong. Certainly some individuals are isolated and have few opportunities for social participation outside the household. Examples include some elderly people who through disability are effectively housebound and some mothers of young children who lack appropriate avenues for social contact. But this state is neither a desired nor a common one. The empirical evidence available indicates that most people do have significant contact with others living outside their household.

An alternative interpretation is that while people are involved in sociable activities with others, the settings for these activities are themselves essentially private ones, the home being particularly important in this. This is a much more interesting argument, which entails a number of elements. To begin with, there are issues about the role of neighbours and neighbourhoods in people's lives. With changes in housing, shopping, and transport, the significance of the neighbourhood for many people has altered. Most, though not all, are less dependent on local ties than in previous times and have little immediate need for extensive co-operation or involvement with the majority of their neighbours. Thus a balance between cordiality and respect for privacy characterizes the majority of these relationships more than extensive sociability or closeness (Bulmer, 1986; Willmott, 1986).

Within this, closer relationships often develop between particular neighbours, with each providing low-level, mundane assistance to the other as necessary. These ties may be more than simply 'good neighbour' ones, over time coming to involve sociability and friendship, though this is by no means inevitable. Where it does happen, interaction is more likely to be based in the home than in the neighbourhood *per se*. That is, the relationship is not in any obvious sense a 'communal' or 'public' one. Even if it involves some activities occurring in neighbourhood settings, it is still developed around the solidarity of the individuals as individuals, rather than being framed by more collective participation, and usually involves socializing in the home.

Questions can also be posed about the extent to which the home actually has replaced public settings for all. For married men there seems little doubt that the home plays a greater part in their leisure activities generally than it did in the earlier part of the twentieth century. But is this so for others? Single men probably lead more 'public' lives than they did in the past, with many regularly using commercial and other public settings for social interaction. Similarly, it would be strange to argue that women's lives, especially married women's lives, have become more privatized over the last two generations (Devine, 1992). Leaving aside changed patterns of employment, which of themselves have fostered informal sociability in both public and private settings, the opportunities available for women to participate in the public realm, informally as well as formally, have been increasing rather than declining.

But equally we can ask how socially significant it actually is if social activities increasingly take place in the home as against more public settings like pubs or social clubs. Does this matter in terms of people's overall social participation? Indeed when, in the past, people met in 'communal' settings, did this necessarily mean that they met 'communally'? Or were they mainly meeting particular others in social spaces which happened to be public rather than private ones? In any case, is having a meal or drinks at home with friends really that different from going to a restaurant or bar with those people?

What this suggests is that the simple distinction between 'public' and 'private' domains is no longer a particularly useful one for understanding people's sociable patterns and the character of their informal ties. Given the major changes there have been in the amenities, facilities, and standards of the home, this arena is now seen as an appropriate one for sociability with a wider range of others than was the case previously. Traditionally, the home has been the place for 'family', especially in working-class culture. Increasingly though, it is accepted as a suitable setting for entertaining and socializing with non-kin. As people spend more of their resources on making the home comfortable and creating the ambience they desire, so the home appears to be opened up to a wider range of 'outsiders'. As Franklin notes in reporting on a study in Bristol, 'The home, far from being an increasingly privatised space, has become an increasingly socialised space' (1989: 111). Certainly the privatization thesis needs to be interpreted with this in mind.

Similar conclusions have been drawn in studies in other societies. For example, on the basis of a study of social networks among a sample of residents in Toronto, Barry Wellman and his associates have argued forcefully that while sociable ties occur far less frequently in public arenas now than is thought to have been the case in the past, this is not the same as people leading isolated lives (Wellman, 1979, 1985; Wellman and Wortley, 1990). For Wellman, the key difference, as above, is that now sociability occurs far more within the home or within other 'non-communal' spaces. But another important aspect of the social networks collected in these Toronto studies concerned the geographical spread of those who were important to the respondents. Although there were differences in this, depending on the work roles of the respondents (Wellman, 1985) and their mobility histories, the main issue was that many of the people included by respondents as important figures in their social networks did not live locally. Consequently meetings between them needed planning; they could not occur haphazardly in local public settings. This is a point that will be discussed more fully in Chapter 9. It is enough here to note again that the way these relationships are organized, especially with respect to the use made of the home, renders simplistic accounts of increased privatization less compelling than they first seem.

Conclusion

This chapter has been concerned with discussing various perspectives on the ways in which the organization of informal relationships have altered with the socio-economic transformations characteristic of late modernity. As we have seen, there are common elements in many popular and academic theories about the destruction of existing solidarities as industrialization developed. Essentially these emphasize the loss of more communally based integration and its replacement by more privatized life-styles. Perhaps inevitably these theories, especially in their popular guises, are rather general. They bring together a range of discrete ideas or strands which need separating. This is certainly true of what is now probably the dominant theoretical perspective on the social changes affecting informal relationships — theories of privatization. In a limited fashion, this chapter has sought to highlight some of these strands inherent in common ideas about the privatization of social life in a way that will inform the analysis of kin and friend ties in the chapters which follow.

It is important to realize that there are no simple answers to the sorts of issue raised in theories, like those of privatization, concerned with the transformation of informal social relationships. Not only is the true history of personal relationships essentially unknowable in the form required, but in any case the theories need to be specified more tightly than is usually the case if they are to be adequately tested. More importantly, social changes to the character of informal solidarities are never uniform. They do not have the same consequences for everyone. Particular economic shifts, for example, may generate fresh opportunities for increased social integration for some groups in society while at the same time dislocating the social lives of others. As argued above, the impact of change on the social networks which particular individuals sustain will depend at least in part on their location within the broader social formation. Such factors as class, gender, geographical mobility, and life-course position will all influence the pattern of social relationships different people sustain with their kin, friends, and other informal contacts.

Further reading

Fiona Devine's book, *Affluent Workers Revisited* (1992), examines the issue of privatization through a restudy of families in Luton, the location of Goldthorpe *et al.*'s original study of privatized workers. In it she considers the theoretical arguments about privatization as well as analysing her own empirical material.

Diana Gittins produces a readable account of the ways family and domestic life have altered over the last century in her book *The Family in Question* (1993), while Graham Crow and Graham Allan analyse developments in community solidarity in *Community Life: An Introduction to Local Social Relationships* (1994).

Chapter Three

Kinship

'How long will it take to get back, Mum?' asked Darren.

'Oh, about another three hours, I suppose, provided we don't get held up too much at those road-works near Birmingham. Did you enjoy yourself?'

'It was OK. I liked seeing Dannie again.'

'Yes,' said Dad, 'you two have always got on well. It's a pity you don't live any closer, so you can see each other a bit more.'

'Why do aunt Anne and uncle Ken live so far away?' said Darren.

'Well, it was mainly because Ken got offered a better job up there, but I think they were looking anyway. Ken was a bit worried about his mum after his dad died. He's not got any brothers or sisters.'

'Gran isn't looking too good, is she?' said Mum.

'No,' said Dad, 'she's very frail, but at least she can still get up and down the stairs.'

'I think she'll move in with Ken and Anne pretty soon,' said Mum.

'Rather them than me,' said Dad.

'Why?' asked Darren.

'Oh, I don't know. It's just never easy having an old person living with you, especially if they need a lot of help. They have their ways of doing things and often they get a bit crotchety if they can't do the things they want to do for themselves.'

'Didn't Gran use to live with us when I was little? That was OK, wasn't it?'

'Well, it was OK,' said Mum, 'but she missed your granddad and we had a few run-ins over this and that. I think it was a bit easier because she was my mum rather than your dad's. But she died not long after she came to us. About eighteen months, wasn't it?'

'Yes, shortly after that second Christmas, remember?' Dad said. 'The one when everything went wrong.'

'Oh yes, burnt turkey and the Christmas tree falling down,' replied Mum.

'I like staying with Dannie. Can we do it again soon?' asked Darren.

'Yes, it's fun,' said Dad. 'It's just such a long way. Oh no. Look at that traffic. I wonder what it is.'

'Didn't Tasha look wonderful at the wedding?' Mum asked. 'They'll certainly have something to remember when they get back from their honeymoon.'

'Where did you say they were going to?' said Darren.

'Florence.'

'Where's that?'

'You know where that is, Darren. It's in Italy,' said Dad.

'Oh yes,' Darren replied. Then he asked, 'Mum, who was that old man in the wheelchair?'

'That was Keith's granddad. His dad's father. How old is he? Did Harold say he was over ninety now?'

'Yeah, ninety-three, I think,' Dad said. 'He was really fit until he had that thrombosis in his leg. He used to walk the half-mile up to Harold's house every day.'

'Is he a relative of mine now?' asked Darren.

'What do you mean?' asked Dad.

'Well, now that Tasha has married Keith, Keith's a relative of mine, isn't he? Does that make all Keith's family my relatives too?'

'Oh, I suppose it does in a sense,' said Dad, 'but I don't know if anyone would really think of it in that way.'

'But Keith's a relative now, isn't he?'

'Yes, he is,' Dad replied. 'He's, er, let's see now. Tasha's your cousin, yes, so I guess he's your cousin-in-law.'

'What's "in-law" mean?'

'It means that he's not related by blood to you, but through marriage,' said Mum.

'So when Keith and Tasha were living together before they got married, was he a relative then?'

'No, not really,' Mum replied, 'though I suppose he was in a way. Tasha and Keith had been living together for, what, three years? That's pretty like a marriage.'

'What about Julie and Frank?' asked Darren. 'They're not married, are they? But they've always lived together.'

'Well, not quite always, but it has been a long time,' said Mum. 'They've had that house since you were four, and with little Sharon now nearly three, it really is as if they are married. Does that make Frank a relative, Gord?'

'I suppose it does. Certainly Sharon is.'

'Sharon's a relative of mine?' asked Darren.

'Yes, of course she is,' Dad replied. 'Julie is Mum's cousin, so that makes Sharon your second cousin.'

'My what?'

'Your second cousin,' Dad repeated.

'What's a second cousin? I've got more than two cousins.'

'No, silly,' said Dad. 'A first cousin is someone who is the child of one of your parents' brothers or sisters. So Dannie is your first cousin, and my nephew. Second cousins are the children of first cousins. So if you and Dannie have children, they would be second cousins. And Julie and Mum are first cousins, so Sharon is your second cousin.'

'Are they?' said Mum. 'I thought they were first cousins once removed. Isn't that what they are?'

'No, they're second cousins,' Dad replied. 'Sharon is your first cousin once removed, not Darren's. Julie's your first cousin, and so Sharon is your first cousin once removed. And if she has children, they would be your first cousins twice removed. And Darren's second cousins once removed. The removed bit means different generations.'

'All this kinship stuff gets a bit complicated, doesn't it?' Mum said.

'Yes,' answered Dad, 'but it doesn't really matter too much, I don't suppose. We only see Julie and Frank at weddings and funerals!'

'What about auntie Margaret? Is she still a relative?' said Darren.

'Well, uncle Andy is,' Dad said. 'But I don't know about Margaret. She was when they were married, but I suppose you stop being a relative once you get divorced. Ben and Tom are still your cousins, but I don't think Margaret counts as a relative any more.'

'Oh look, there's been a crash!' Mum exclaimed. 'That's what's been holding us up. It doesn't look as though anyone got hurt.'

'No,' said Dad, 'but look at the front of that car. That's taken a bit of damage.'

'And is nana Jo a relative?' asked Darren.

'Yes, of course she is . . . Though I suppose you could say she's not a real relative,' Dad replied. 'You've always known her as your nana, but she's not really your nana, is she? After my mum and dad got divorced, and Dad married Jo, she became my stepmother, though I never lived with them. I'd left home by the time Dad remarried, and I can't say we got on very well to begin with. I suppose technically she's your step-grandmother. Does that make her a relative? I reckon it does.'

This story of a family returning home from a wedding and puzzling over who counts as a relative illustrates a number of features of kinship in contemporary Britain. Aside from the complications — caused by changing patterns of family formation and dissolution — cohabitation, divorce, and stepfamilies, in particular — it indicates the extent to

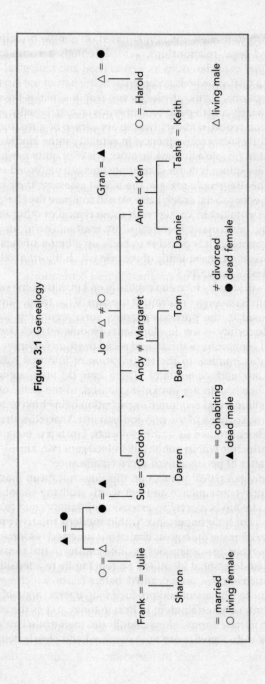

Figure 3.1 Genealogy

which kinship, though apparently based on simple principles of biological and legal relationships, actually entails a complex of social and personal considerations as well as legal and biological ones. Who counts as a relative, who is accepted as being part of the kin group, and what obligations, rights, privileges, and responsibilities flow from this, vary very widely and depend on numerous factors. Equally, while in the conversation reported above, kinship appears to be a matter of interest but with little social consequence, in actuality some kin ties are highly significant in people's lives while other ones are quite peripheral. This section will explore how these relationships are patterned socially, examining the use people make of them, and assessing their importance within the wider social order. Later we will compare the character of the solidarities entailed in kin ties with those typical of other informal relationships, particularly friendships. By examining the social basis of these different ties it is possible to build up a better understanding of their nature and consequently of the role which informal relationships in general play in our lives.

But we will start by focusing explicitly on kinship. Some might argue that kinship is no longer relevant at the turn of the twenty-first century. As was noted in the previous chapter, such arguments have a long history. Modernity — the development of industrial societies with their associated economic, political, and social transformations — has often been seen as inimical to the continuation of informal solidarities of both kinship and community. There can be little argument that countries like Britain are not kinship-based, in the sense of the main forms of political and economic organization being built around ties of kinship. Unlike many of the non-industrialized societies that have traditionally been studied by anthropologists, kinship is not a central organizing principle within public life. Indeed generally kinship is seen as more a matter of personal than social significance.

Yet as Morgan (1975) points out, this does not mean that kinship is really of little consequence and not worth studying sociologically. At one level, kinship is merely an extension of 'family', and to argue that family life is of little importance within modern society would be absurd. Many of us devote a great deal of our time and resources to family matters, perceiving our families as quite central in the construction of our social and personal identities. So too, family relationships are the topic of much interest, gossip, and debate, a lesson which is well recognized by those who script and produce soap operas, arguably the most popular form of entertainment in Britain today. Yet as the car-journey discussion narrated above shows, family ties merge into kinship ones in a seamless web. Families are not contained and clearly defined units.

Rather the category 'family' is variable; we mean different things by the term in different contexts. 'My family' may mean my partner and dependent children. It may mean my children from more than one marriage. It may include my parents; possibly, on occasion, even my siblings, aunts and uncles, or parents-in-law. Indeed by focusing on kinship rather than family, some of these contextual ambiguities disappear. More importantly, by making kinship the concern, we can begin to see where the boundaries are drawn around different collectivities of relatives who may on different occasions and with different strengths be thought of as 'family'.

The issue, in other words, is partly to do with who it is we regard as relatives — who we recognize as having a 'family' link with us; who we include within our 'kin set'. As we shall see later, this question was one which was focal to some of the earlier kinship studies undertaken in Britain, especially by Raymond Firth and his colleagues (Firth, 1956; Firth *et al.*, 1970). Equally though, we need to be concerned with the social consequences of such recognition. That is, what follows from being a relative — what demands can we make of our relatives; what obligations do we owe them; what is the character of the exchanges which typify different relationships? This raises a further set of questions about the extent to which there is variation in the way we treat different relatives. Do we, for example, treat all aunts or all cousins in the same way? Are we equally obligated to them all? If there are differences, how do we explain these?

Moreover, do different people treat the same category of relative in an equivalent way? Here the question is whether it is appropriate to regard contemporary Britain as having a more or less uniform kinship system. Again, this issue was one which has been important in kinship studies over the last forty years. Essentially, when anthropologists studied small-scale, non-industrialized societies, they were able to unpick the fabric of social organization by focusing on kinship. Because of the centrality of kinship in all aspects of life in these societies, a full appreciation of the kinship system allowed the social and economic structure to be understood and explained. The question which obviously arose was how these arrangements differed from those found in industrial societies. Did industrial societies recognize the same range of kinship? Were there systematic ways of treating different categories of kin? Did we have a kinship system as such, or merely a range of individualized options with each person responding to kin in a piecemeal and disorganized fashion? And if there was a kinship system as such, how did this influence and respond to the changes which were occurring in production with the development of industrialization and market capitalism?

The tradition of British kinship studies

Some of these issues will be addressed in the next chapter. Here we will focus on the broad ways in which kinship studies have developed in Britain over the last forty or so years. As noted already, much of the early analysis of kinship was conducted by anthropologists or by sociologists who were much influenced by anthropological concerns. In particular, anthropologists conducting research into a range of different substantive topics in Britain frequently included an account of kinship relations in their monographs. Although actually conducted in Eire, one of the most influential early studies was undertaken by Arensberg and Kimball (1940), on family farming in County Clare. As part of this rural community study, Arensberg and Kimball focused on the operation of family and kinship ties within the agricultural economy, and showed how significant kinship was for interpreting the dominant forms of social and economic organization. Far from being redundant or residual, kinship, and in particular the control which older generations maintained over those from younger generations who remained in the locality, seemed central to the continuation of the form of life found amongst farming families in the area.

Other rural community studies followed the lead given by Arensberg and Kimball. In 1950, Rees published his study of Llanfihangel, a parish in mid-Wales. He too illustrated how kinship ties were fully integrated into the social and economic life of this farming community. Frankenberg (1957) produced a further study of a farming locality, Glynceiriog on the Welsh border, once again indicating that family and kinship ties were significant in helping sustain the community's organization and thus, from the analyst's perspective, in revealing the ways in which community co-operations and tensions were managed. One of the first comparable English studies was undertaken by Williams (1956) in Gosforth, in what is now Cumbria. This, too, was a community study of an agriculturally dominated locality, though one based on a market town rather than a more isolated rural setting. Williams was especially concerned with social stratification, so that as well as examining the kinship system in operation in Gosforth for its own sake he also traced how it interacted with the creation and maintenance of wealth through land-owning. He was able to demonstrate clearly that kinship ties were used extensively in efforts to protect the material interests of farming families. Williams (1963) followed his Gosforth research with a study of a rather different rural community, Ashworthy in Devon, in which the collection of kinship data played an even larger part.

It could be commented that, given all these studies were of rural communities, it is not really that surprising that kinship ties were of consequence. Aside from the relatively small scale of such communities, which can often result in quite extensive local kinship networks, the centrality of land within agricultural production has consequences for the character of intergenerational relationships. That is, as Arensberg and Kimball (1940) forcefully demonstrated, when the generations are dependent for their income, well-being, and life-style on 'family' property, the control of that property can influence kin relationships in significant ways. (For a general discussion of property and family solidarity see Allan, 1982.)

Surely the position in urban localities was likely to be rather different? It was in these areas that the impact of industrialization and modernity was likely to be greatest, as factors like geographical mobility, individual wage-labour, and domestic privatization undermined the types of kinship solidarity found in rural communities. Yet as studies of kinship in urban areas developed in Britain, they too showed that the death of kinship had been overexaggerated in popular theorizing. To begin with, there was the evidence produced in the growing number of urban community studies undertaken by sociologists in the 1950s and early 1960s. In particular, the work of those associated with the Institute of Community Studies in Bethnal Green, London demonstrated that kinship was alive and well, being used as a major resource for coping with life's many contingencies. The classic studies here were Young and Willmott's *Family and Kinship in East London* (1957) and Townsend's *The Family Life of Old People* (1963), both of which highlighted the significance of kin ties in the construction of their respondents' everyday lives. The picture that emerged from these various studies was that in 'traditional working class communities' (Crow and Allan, 1994), kinship support was an unremarkable, largely taken-for-granted feature of people's routine activities. Rather than being insulated in tightly bound nuclear households, many people were part of quite large and extensive local kinship networks, with different relatives being drawn on as appropriate to facilitate people's different agendas.

But as well as these urban and rural community studies, which in analysing different aspects of social, economic, and political organization demonstrated the continuing significance of kin relationships in people's everyday lives, a small number of studies emerged in the post-war period which focused more specifically on kinship as their major topic. Three were particularly important and are worth discussing in more detail here. They are Firth's *Two Studies of Kinship in London* (1956); Rosser and Harris's *The Family and Social Change* (1965, reprinted in 1983); and Firth, Hubert, and Forge's *Families and their Relatives* (1970).

In the first of these books, Firth reports on two studies he and his colleagues conducted in the 1940s and 1950s into the kin relationships maintained by two samples of respondents in London. The main study was of 'South Borough', in which respondents were drawn from the residents of a block of flats in a working-class area of south London. On the basis of extensive interviews, Firth, like those other researchers enquiring into working-class kinship at the time, was struck by the vibrancy of kin ties amongst his sample. While recognizing that the kinship system being studied was quite different from those found in the non-industrial 'kinship'-oriented societies which were the core focus of much anthropological research, he nonetheless demonstrated that the knowledge of kinship which people had was far more extensive than common theorizing at the time suggested. People may not have known a great deal about their more distant ancestors — there were few, for example, who could trace their lineage back further than their grandparents — but they did have quite extensive knowledge of contemporary kin. Equally, a portion of these kin, though not the majority, were significant figures in their social lives.

In this monograph, Firth began to develop a classificatory schema for categorizing kin. The first stage of this was to map out his respondents' genealogies. In doing this, he was, of course, discovering much about the ways in which his respondents drew boundaries around kinship and where kinship 'stopped' — whether, for example, second cousins were recognized as kin; whether kin who were now dead were still seen as kin; whether in-laws were included as kin, and if so, which ones. In those households where kinship knowledge was studied in depth, Firth reports that on average 146 kin were recognized, ranging from 37 to 246 (1956: 38). While there is a good deal of variability between households, knowledge of kinship rarely extended beyond second cousins. Once the genealogies were collected, Firth was then able to analyse the social consequences of kinship recognition and specify what sorts of relationships people developed with different categories of kin. By examining his respondents' kinship organization in this way, he was able to indicate the range of social relationships which developed as well as examine the broad similarities there were in the treatment of kin.

In his second, much fuller study Firth and his colleagues concentrated on middle-class kinship. They examined the kinship ties, attitudes, and behaviour of a sample of middle-class households, from two areas of London. The findings here were broadly similar to those of the first study. While most people knew relatively little about the generations before their grandparents, they did generally have knowledge of first cousins and genealogically closer relatives, and on occasion of other, more distant kin. In this study, Firth, Hubert, and Forge were able to provide a good deal of detail about the dynamics of kin relationships, the types of solidarity that developed, and the conflicts that arose. As with the earlier study, what emerged was a much broader knowledge of kinship than they had expected to find. These respondents recognized an average of 84 kin, ranging from 7 to 388. This is broadly similar to the numbers in Firth's first study, allowing for the fact that in the former study the household rather than the individual was the unit used in constructing the genealogies. The second study also supported the idea developed in the first that while kinship ties were, to use Firth's terms, quite 'permissive' (Firth *et al.*, 1970: 453) — kinship behaviour appeared to be relatively freely chosen rather than tightly prescribed by social norms, conventions, or rules — in practice, there were few people who did not have a degree of interest in kinship matters and whose lives were unaffected by solidarities with kin living outside the household.

On the basis of these two studies, Firth and his colleagues developed a four-level classification of kinship involvement (see Figure 3.2). While, given the important demographic shifts that have occurred in Britain in the years since the fieldwork was conducted, Firth's studies may now be regarded as of historical rather than contemporary interest, this classification scheme is still useful for sorting out the social significance of different categories of kin. (For full details of this, see ibid. 154–8.)

The first level of classification is 'recognized kin'. Essentially this refers to all the kin which a person acknowledges as existing, the person's

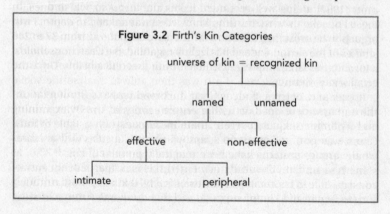

Figure 3.2 Firth's Kin Categories

universe of kin = recognized kin

named   unnamed

effective   non-effective

intimate   peripheral

kin universe — those who are included in the genealogies which people construct. These recognized kin can then be subdivided into those who are known by name (referred to as 'nominated' kin in the earlier study) and those who are not. A respondent may know, for example, that a grandmother had a sister but not know the name of that sister. Or someone may recollect that a cousin had three children, two boys and a girl, but not know their names or any other details about them. The simple idea here is that if people do not know the name of a kinsperson, that person is unlikely to be of consequence in their lives. Named kin can in turn be divided into 'effective' and 'non-effective' kin. The former are those with whom you have some form of social contact, the latter those with whom you rarely or never interact. Finally, effective kin can be separated into 'intimate' and 'peripheral' kin. 'Intimate' kin are those who you see regularly and who play a significant role in your life, those where contact is 'purposeful, close and frequent' (ibid. 156).

While very simple, separating kin in these ways is actually quite helpful in revealing the parameters of kinship. It easily and quickly allows you to see which kin are important socially, what differences there are between the same genealogical categories of kin, and how the kinship system is structured. In this, it is no more than a starting-point, but one which is useful in helping to frame appropriate questions. We will take up some of these issues in the next chapter.

Rosser and Harris's (1965) study was quite different to Firth's two. Theirs was a direct response to the work of the Institute of Community Studies in London's East End. They wanted to examine whether the patterns of familial and kinship involvement in other urban areas were similar to those found in Bethnal Green, especially by Young and Willmott (1957). Being well-grounded in both anthropological and sociological perspectives, their study, which was undertaken in Swansea, was arguably the most insightful and informative of all the kinship-oriented studies of the period. Indeed it is rightly regarded as a classic example of a locality-based kinship study which is both theoretically informed and empirically rigorous.

Rosser and Harris's study echoed the broad range of findings about the importance of close kin within people's everyday lives which Young and Willmott had uncovered, thereby demonstrating that Bethnal Green was not, in Townsend's famous phrase, 'a sub-cultural island where strange customs have been magically preserved' (1963: 236), as some had hinted. The study cemented the idea that kinship was of consequence in contemporary British society, that people did routinely turn to family and kin for support, and that there was a much broader interest in, and commitment to, the idea of kinship than theories of modernization suggested.

At the same time, they recognized that kinship was not a central element in the social formation. At a structural level, the core component of modern, industrial societies lies in the economic sphere. Kinship is not unimportant or completely detached from this, but it is relatively marginal to it (Rosser and Harris, 1965: 287–8). Social organization, in other words, is not explicable in terms of kinship. It is a different matter, however, at an individual level, where kin ties are often significant both in terms of social identification and social support. Importantly, though, it is not all kin ties which are significant, and nor is it a fixed, socially specified group of kin who matter. As Rosser and Harris write:

it is essential to see it [the extended family] as an enduring social *entity* — the elementary family writ large — and not as a precisely defined social group based on proximity of residence or on an arbitrarily-determined high frequency of face-to-face contact. We have described it rather as a variable, amorphous,

---

Activity 3.1 Constructing your own Genealogy

Write out your own genealogy. You will get an idea of how this can be done by looking at Figure 3.1. Do this on your own to begin with and see how full a genealogy you can construct. Think about how you are defining kinship, who you are excluding, where you see your kinship network's boundaries being drawn. Once you have done this, try to use Firth's classifications to specify the social significance in your life of the different kin you have included.

Once you have done this, do the same for one or both of your parents. Start from scratch and see what genealogies they are able to construct. You can then do the same for one or more of your grandparents. While you are doing this, listen to the stories they tell you about their relationships with different kin. How have these changed over time? What patterns can you see in these changes? How do their kin universes compare with yours and with your parent(s)?

One of the difficulties you are likely to face is representing all the kin ties you have on a single sheet of paper. This becomes especially difficult if there are a number of divorces and remarriages among your kin group. It may be necessary for you to 'block' certain parts of the genealogy and reproduce them separately on a new page, or alternatively in a boxed section of the main genealogy. You are likely to find that producing 'tidy' genealogical diagrams is not as simple as it first seems!

---

vague social grouping within which circulate — often over great distances — strong sentiments of belonging (ibid. 288; emphasis in the original).

That is, who belongs to this 'social entity' is neither static nor uniform; its boundaries are permeable, depending on the circumstances in which individuals, couples, and elementary families find themselves. Its membership — and even this term implies too strong a boundary around it — is liable to change over time as people's interests and commitments, both inside and outside the family sphere, alter. In particular, its make-up changes as people move through the life-course, adopting new roles and developing their relationships in different ways. It is in this sense that Rosser and Harris (ibid. 200) refer to kinship as 'essentially a process'.

Following Rosser and Harris's important work, other researchers also used Swansea as a base for studying kinship patterns. Two studies were particularly interesting in showing how material and economic assets were used to cement kin relationships. Colin Bell (1968), in a study of young middle-class couples, built on Rosser and Harris's concern for the tensions between the couple's two natal families. Whereas Rosser and Harris (1965: 289) had argued that the key kinship linkage typically consisted of wife's mother–wife–husband–husband's mother, Bell found that fathers played a significant role among his middle-class sample because of the material advantages that often flowed through them. In particular he demonstrated how middle-class fathers used their available resources to ensure their children sustained an appropriately middle-class life-style, pointing out that gifts to grandchildren were frequently used as a means of doing this without threatening the valued independence of the younger couple. In the process, though, what the older generation was doing was helping ensure that it maintained an active relationship with the younger generations.

In the second study, Leonard (1980) examined engagement and marriage practices among a sample of young people from a broadly similar perspective to Bell's. Her interest was in the routine generosity that parents, and in particular the bride's mother, showed to their children at this time, arguing that their 'spoiling' of their children was more than simply the expression of love and concern. It was a means by which mothers attempted to ensure a continued relationship with their daughters as the latter left the parental home to form their own new families. In recognizing their mother's generosity, the daughters were intrinsically accepting the right of their mothers to continue to be involved in their lives. That is, by giving as they did, the mothers created a sense of obligation in their daughters which served to reduce the

Figure 3.3 Selected British Kinship Studies

1950	A. Rees	*Life in a Welsh Countryside*
1956	R. Firth	*Two Studies of Kinship in London*
1956	J. Mogey	*Family and Neighbourhood*
1957	M. Young and P. Willmott	*Family and Kinship in East London*
1958	P. Townsend	*The Family Life of Old People*
1960	P. Willmott and M. Young	*Family and Class in a London Suburb*
1965	C. Rosser and C. Harris	*The Family and Social Change*
1968	C. Bell	*Middle Class Families*
1970	R. Firth, J. Hubert, and A. Forge	*Families and their Relatives*
1979	G. Allan	*A Sociology of Friendship and Kinship*
1980	D. Leonard	*Sex and Generation*
1981	M. Strathern	*Kinship at the Core*
1989	J. Finch	*Family Obligations and Social Change*
1989	M. Grieco	*Keeping it in the Family*
1989	H. Qureshi and A. Walker	*The Caring Relationship*
1993	J. Finch and J. Mason	*Negotiating Family Responsibilities*

potential schisms generated during this disruptive family phase. Thus both Bell's and Leonard's studies are significant for highlighting the role which material resources can play in helping to sustain kinship solidarity across generations.

Conclusion

Even from this preliminary discussion of the social basis of kinship, it is evident that kin relationships are more complicated than we often assume. Indeed, since the writing of the reports discussed in this chapter, the character of kinship bonds has become even more complex, as a consequence of the higher incidence in contemporary society of cohabitation, divorce, and remarriage. Yet unfortunately our knowledge of kinship in Britain has not developed in response to these changes. There are a number of studies which relate to particular aspects of familial and kinship behaviour, but very few which focus explicitly on the social basis of kinship in the way in which the main studies introduced here did. Indeed, like locality and community studies, kinship studies became somewhat unfashionable in the 1970s and 1980s. Perhaps because of the very success of the body of research developed in the previous twenty years, it seemed few sociologists were attracted to explore this topic further. Even some of the kinship reports which were published in the 1980s (e.g. Leonard, 1980; Strathern, 1981) were actually based on research conducted in the 1960s.

And it is important to recognize just how successful much of the kinship research undertaken around this period actually was. Whatever criticisms can be made of the different studies, and as with all empirical research it is not hard to find 'flaws' within them, the work demonstrated quite clearly that the era's moral panics about the decline of kinship solidarities were misplaced. Collectively it highlighted the continued significance of specific kin ties in people's lives, even while recognizing that at a societal level kin relationships as such were not of great structural consequence. Even in this, though, later work was able to demonstrate that aspects of some kin ties served to protect the economic and social standing of those involved. The significance of this aspect of kinship had become clear in some of the élite studies which were being published (in particular, see Lupton and Wilson, 1959), but by the end of the decade the contribution which kinship made to the well-being of other social groups was also better understood. In the three chapters which follow, the aim will be to build on the foundation laid in these now classic works on kinship, examining some of the changes which have occurred and considering more fully the social basis of kinship solidarity and conflict.

Further reading

The Family and Social Change (1965, 1983) by Colin Rosser and Chris Harris is the most sociologically sophisticated of the kinship studies which were produced in the 1950s and 1960s, a key period in the development of British kinship research. Republished in 1983, it is still well worth reading.

The other classic book of the period is Michael Young and Peter Willmott's *Family and Kinship in East London* (1957), which has become the most-read kinship study produced in Britain. As a major influence on much later research and for the flavour it gives of working-class kinship in the immediate post-war period, it continues to warrant attention.

Chapter Four

A Kinship System?

In the last chapter, Firth's research into people's kinship knowledge and interactions was introduced. The idea of different cultures having distinct kinship systems was also raised. In this chapter, we shall build on Firth's work to see whether it is reasonable to talk about a British kinship system, and if so what the characteristics of that system are. Firth's work is now of course rather dated. The purpose in discussing it is not to suggest that kinship patterns have remained unaltered, but rather to use his work as a base for raising a series of questions about the nature of kinship in contemporary Britain. A number of these questions will be addressed in this chapter. Others will be dealt with more fully in the two following chapters.

What is a kinship system?

Before deciding whether or not modern Britain can be characterized as having a kinship system, it is first necessary to consider what this term means. How can we recognize whether a kinship system exists? What is it that characterizes such a system and warrants the label 'system'? A number of different answers can be given to these questions. To begin with, for a kinship system to be operating there needs to be a broad consistency in the patterns of relationship which exist between different kin. This does not mean that all kin, or all those included within a given category of kinship, will be treated equivalently, but it does mean that there will be agreement about what is appropriate for given relationships and what is inappropriate. Variation can occur, and importantly some of that variation will be structured around significant social divisions as well as personal preference. Thus there may be differences in the kin behaviour of people with different characteristics — being male or female, for example, or being of a particular age —

vis-à-vis categories of kinship. The expectations there are of these people, the demands they experience as legitimate, the commitments they have may vary systematically. Such differences themselves can be built into the overarching kinship system.

Equally, though, there can be structured differences in kinship behaviour which reflect not just differences in the social expectations of actors with different characteristics, but also the existence of more than one distinct kinship system. It could for example be that working-class kinship — however class is defined — is routinely patterned in a different way to middle- or upper-class kinship. Equally, and arguably more pertinent within contemporary Britain, it may be that quite discrete kinship systems are found amongst different ethnic groups. There has been debate, for example, over the similarities and differences of 'English' and 'Afro-Caribbean' kinship. Equally, the kinship obligations and commitments of ethnic 'Asian' individuals and families in Britain are frequently portrayed as being different to those of the majority population. We will consider the empirical arguments about these matters later. Here it is sufficient to note that like all discussions of culture and cultural difference, it is in practice extremely difficult to draw boundaries around cultural or subcultural groups. Membership is rarely that clear-cut; what counts as sufficiently different to constitute a cultural boundary in a multicultural society like contemporary Britain is an analytical matter lying in the eye of the analyst as well as in empirical reality.

Furthermore, in looking at the existence or otherwise of kinship system(s), it can be recognized that different criteria can be brought into play. At one level, we could focus on behaviour — what people actually do with different kin; the exchanges they are involved in; and the organization of their interactions. Equally, though, we may focus on their beliefs, either in general about the way they think kinship should normally be patterned or more specifically about the commitments and obligations they feel towards their own particular kin. In reality, an analysis of kinship is rightly concerned with all these issues. It is not just behaviour that counts, nor is it just the idealized model of kinship to which people claim to subscribe. Rather, to understand kinship and assess whether a kinship system exists, it is necessary to relate these different factors together and see how kinship beliefs interact with commitment and expressed solidarity. The problem of boundaries and difference remain, and indeed become more complex as individual circumstances are added to the picture as factors which influence the ways in which belief, behaviour, and commitment are articulated in reality.

The relationship between these different aspects of kinship will be explored below as we try to uncover the ways in which kinship operates. Let us set the scene now, though, by focusing on the parameters of kinship behaviour, starting with Raymond Firth's studies of kinship in London. As we have seen, Firth and his colleagues distinguished between kin not in genealogical terms but on the basis of the personal relationships which respondents maintained with their different kin. He categorized kin as named or not, effective, and intimate. Although, or perhaps because, this classification is simple, it does allow us to see which kin are significant in people's lives, what variation there is in the relationships which are developed between different genealogical kin, and whether the differences there are are systematically structured by identifiable economic and social factors.

The Firth studies

Before discussing Firth's findings, there are two issues of clarification which are worth highlighting. First, in what follows I shall use Firth's terms 'exclusively' rather than 'inclusively'. That is, while effective kin are also by definition named kin, I shall use the term 'named kin' below to mean those who are only in the named category and not in the effective one. Similarly, in referring to 'effective kin' I shall mean those who are not also 'intimate kin'. Secondly, it is helpful to distinguish 'primary' kin from 'secondary' kin. Unlike Firth's terms, which are socially derived, these are genealogical categories. They refer to the closeness of the genealogical link between two kin. Primary kin are those who are connected by just one genealogical link to one another; that is, they are parents, siblings, and children. Secondary kin are all other kin, that is those within the genealogy whose connection to one another is through at least one intermediary kinsperson. Thus, for example, an aunt and a niece are secondary kin, being linked through, say, the sister-mother tie. Cousins, grandparents, aunts, and uncles all form part of a person's secondary kin set.

What is evident from Firth's studies is that those who are only named kin are, in the great majority of cases, secondary kin. Obvious though this appears, given people's knowledge of kinship in contemporary Britain, it is worth emphasizing. Primary kin ties only rarely break down completely to the extent that there is no social contact whatsoever. While relationships may not be harmonious, while there may be misgivings, recriminations, and dislike between primary kin, these features do not usually mean that the relationship itself becomes empty. They may not all be the relationships we want, but they are nonetheless usually sustained in some form. Thus in Firth *et al.*'s (1970) study of middle-class kinship, in only 3 cases (out of 168) was there no contact between a parent and their adult child. Similarly only 7 per cent of sibling relationships were classified as 'negative' (rather than positive or indifferent) (ibid. 401, 430).

In some cases, lack of contact is the result of the individual involved having been separated from their birth family in childhood. Sometimes a rift is caused through major arguments, with inheritance issues appearing to loom large in such cases. It can also result from tension arising between in-laws; a person in conflict with their sibling's spouse, for example, may have little contact with that sibling. Parental divorce is also responsible for the breakdown of some relationships, particularly where the separation has been acrimonious. Given the recent increases there have been in levels of divorce, such cases will now be much more common. Here it needs remembering that up to 50 per cent of children lose effective contact with their non-residential parent within a few years of their parents' divorce.

But if, by and large, named kin are confined to secondary kin, which secondary kin in particular? Are all secondary kin as liable to be in the named category as one another? As would be expected, the answer to this is 'no'. Some secondary kin are far more likely to be placed in this category, or indeed not even be named, than others. Specifically, the more distant the genealogical tie, the less tends to be known about them. So typically, aunts, and uncles, as well as grandparents and primary kin, are found in the effective or intimate kin sets, but the likelihood of first cousins being included is significantly less. In Firth *et al.*'s study of middle-class kinship, their respondents had no contact at all with 40 per cent of their first cousins, and only saw a further 45 per cent rarely, for example at family ceremonies (ibid. 447). More genealogically distant cousins rarely make it into the intimate or effective sets, and, as mentioned in the previous chapter, when such kin are known about, few details about them tend to be remembered.

In Firth's studies, grandparents, aunts, and uncles were normally included in the effective kin set, while first cousins were split between named and effective kin. This category of 'effective kin' involves social activity, but it must be remembered that this is not always purposeful. That is, some of these kin relationships are activated as a consequence of events which have not been organized specifically in order to further this particular tie. For example, some kin are met on 'kin occasions', such as weddings and funerals, and perhaps Christmas or other religious ceremonies, not with the deliberate intent of meeting these particular kin, but because both sides happen to go to the same events because of their kinship linkage. The story at the beginning of Chapter 3 is not untypical of this.

Moreover, some kin may be met more regularly, but again not through conscious planning (Strathern, 1981). For example, aunts or cousins may be met because they happen to be visiting your parents at the same time you are. At one level, these meetings appear to be chance affairs. However, the situation is generally more complex than this, especially when these kin ties are more rather than less significant to those involved. Rather than just 'happening', there is often an element of planning and co-ordination built into them even though circumstance continues to play a large part. Thus, for example, when an adult child living some distance away visits their parents' home (say, with their family), they may meet aunts, uncles, or cousins through their parents arranging for these people to visit at the time. Think here about the people who are seen at times of religious celebration such as Christmas, Diwali, or *Eid*. These often involve occasions where such interactions occur, whether or not they have been deliberately arranged with meeting specific kin in mind.

The term 'structured chance' has been used to refer to these kinds of interactions which tend not to be deliberately planned, yet to involve more than just 'chance' (Allan, 1979). Often what is important in them is that they stem from the interconnections which kinship routinely involves. In particular, because kinship involves a set, or network, of relationships rather than just individual ties, the relationships often arise as a consequence of kinship's 'network' implications rather than simply through 'individual' intention. In social action the genealogy is not just a diagram of those linked by blood or marriage, but becomes a social network in which intermediary kin can play a significant part in keeping the relationships between more distant kin active.

As well as facilitating contact in ways similar to those illustrated above, intermediary kin also act as news and gossip conduits, passing on information about different kin members' activities and keeping people up to date with each other's news. While the issue does not appear to have been studied systematically, from everyday experience it seems that the routine discussion of the current circumstances and activities of various kin forms a significant part of much kin interaction. It thus helps to keep relationships 'active' even when there is little contact. It is in this sense that kinship needs to be understood as a social network, a matter to which we shall return later in this chapter.

Secondary kin

In some ways a convenient image of kinship solidarity and commitment is that of an onion (Parsons, 1943). If the individual (or couple or nuclear family) is regarded as the middle or the core, each layer of the onion can be regarded as the next layer of genealogically more distant kin. Those closest to the centre, primary kin, and then the other primary kin of one's own primary kin, are the ones with whom there is likely to be most involvement and generally most attachment. Although too ego-centred — there is after all no real centre to a kinship genealogy — this image usefully highlights the connections there are within kinship. Just as each layer of the onion is bound to the ones next to it, so the kinship genealogy extends outwards, relating people to one another (in both the kinship and non-kinship sense of this term), though the more distant the onion layer the less close the social ties generally are.

However, such an image is by no means complete. It is clear from the early kinship studies like Firth's that the genealogy cannot be translated in a mechanical fashion into a social network. Some secondary kin are important figures in the individual's landscape, often though not always because their ties with intermediate kin have been particularly strong. Sometimes primary kin are, or become, comparatively insignificant. Circumstances, including geographical mobility and changes in life-course experiences, can play a large part in this. On occasion too, particular kin who previously have played a very minor, or even non-existent, part in one's life can become of greater consequence. Particularly interesting examples of this often seem to arise when people migrate to a new area.

Rosser and Harris (1965: 229) provide an apt, though perhaps a slightly extreme, illustration of this in their discussion of Donald. Donald was a nephew of one of Rosser and Harris's respondents, who for work reasons had to move from his home in Bolton to work in the Swansea area. Although there had been no contact for some thirty years before this, his aunt offered to put Donald up for the four months he was working in the area. Such examples of individuals discovering they have cousins or other kin, about whom they perhaps have never previously heard a great deal, in areas to which they are about to move seems surprisingly common. There are two points about it which are worth highlighting.

First, it again illustrates the network aspect of kinship (Grieco, 1987). Individuals hear through their parents or other intermediaries of people to whom they can recognize a kin link even though that kin link has never been one which they have previously activated. The kin involved may not even have been in each other's 'named' category before changed circumstance made them more pertinent. Second, and more importantly, it indicates the extent to which kinship can act as a resource. In the case of Donald, it was regarded as acceptable to turn to kin, even where there had been little previous direct involvement, to seek support. The outcome in Donald's instance — living with the relatives for quite a long period — was quite extreme, but the idea of using them to help him establish himself in a new area was not.

One issue here concerns the range of kin of whom favours can be asked. When does genealogical distance make it problematic to ask them for assistance? Another question is whether kin have some degree of obligation to provide support or whether it is a matter of individual volition. As we shall see in Chapter 6 when we look at more recent research into kinship obligation, these issues are not straightforward. Suffice it to say here that generally it is not simply a matter of genealogical closeness. Individual circumstance is also of consequence, and, more importantly, in most instances the social ties which have been maintained between intermediary kin do influence the implicit negotiations which develop around kinship support and favours.

In summary, what the various kinship studies have demonstrated is that primary kin generally remain important in people's lives, but that involvement with secondary kin is typically much more varied. Kin relationships are not 'rule-governed', tending in Firth's terms to be 'permissive' rather than 'obligatory' (1956: 14), but certain patterns in the structuring of these relationships emerge quite consistently. First, there is a tailing-off of commitment with genealogical distance. Second, the character of the relationships maintained with kin is influenced by circumstance, and in particular by the network consequences of kinship as a genealogical system. Often relationships cannot be understood properly in isolation; what also matters is the nature of the relationships which are maintained by intermediate kin. In a variety of ways these shape the resultant secondary kin tie. And thirdly, kinship does act as a resource for people. This occurs at a routine and daily level with some primary kin especially, but interestingly, more genealogically and socially distant kin can also be turned to at times for specific forms of support relevant to their circumstances. While the solidarity of kin groups is not as marked as it is in some other societies, such as those for example in southern Europe (Peristiany, 1976), nonetheless these actions demonstrate that kinship solidarity plays a part in the social worlds most people construct.

Changes

As noted, many of the key kinship studies are now quite old. For instance, though Firth's second study was published in 1970, the fieldwork for it was undertaken in the early 1960s. Britain's economic and social climate has changed quite significantly since that time, with implications for family and domestic life, and consequently in principle for the way in which kinship is organized. Such matters as the sexual freedoms established in the 1960s; the rise in levels of divorce since the early 1970s together with growth in the number of lone-parent households and stepfamilies; Britain's development as a far more multicultural society than in mid-century; changed patterns of cohabitation over the period; quite radical shifts in patterns of housing tenure; increases in economic insecurity and unemployment have all potentially had an impact on the ways in which kinship ties are organized.

Yet these kinship studies have not been directly replicated in recent times. While many studies contain reference to kin behaviour, only quite rarely has kinship as such been the focus of research. In general, rather more attention has been paid to the operation of households than to wider kin relations. A notable exception here is the research conducted by Janet Finch, Jennifer Mason, and their colleagues (Finch, 1989; Finch and Mason, 1993). This work will be discussed more fully in Chapter 6. However, much of what the research of a generation ago deduced about the character of British kinship still seems to hold, at least in broad terms, in contemporary Britain. The emphasis on primary over secondary kinship remains, and in particular the commitment across generations. For instance, despite the claims at times made by politicians and other pundits, there is little evidence to suggest that there has been dramatic change in the care and support kin provide one another. On occasion secondary kin are important in people's lives, but secondary kin in the 'intimate' category are generally few in number. Most secondary kin do not have very active relationships with one another. Where they do there are normally specific reasons for this, often involving the strength of the intermediary primary kin ties.

However, there are three particular developments occurring over the last thirty or so years that warrant special mention, as they have each led to the picture portrayed in the earlier kinship studies needing to be modified. They are, first, changed patterns of housing allocation and geographical mobility; second, altered household and family forms;

and third, the growth of ethnic diversity. Each will be discussed briefly here in turn.

Housing allocation and geographical mobility

The ways in which housing is allocated have changed dramatically in the course of this century, with quite significant consequences for kinship interaction. For the first half of this century private renting was the predominant form of housing. This meant that kin frequently lived close to one another, as local connections were often crucial in acquiring this housing. Mothers, for example, would push their newly married children's case with the local rent collector, finding out what property was becoming vacant and arguing to have their children housed there. Inside knowledge mattered, as did the family's reputation as good tenants.

As owner-occupation and local authority housing developed, the likelihood of being housed near to parents and siblings diminished. Certainly the local connection still mattered in the case of local authority housing, but, especially with post-war redevelopment programmes, available housing tended not to be very close to those areas in which people previously lived. Moreover, the development of new educational opportunities in the 1950s and 1960s was associated with increased levels of social mobility. Often this entailed an element of geographical mobility too, so that again kin groups were less likely to be living close together.

There has been much debate in the literature on the kinship consequences of these changes. Clearly geographical separation makes some forms of kinship co-operation impossible. If you live a distance away from people, you cannot provide the same type of support as you can if you live within walking distance. In particular, help with the more or less routine contingencies of daily living is not possible. It also renders help with, say, acute or chronic illness difficult. But we still need to ask the question of whether the relationship which people typically have with their kin is actually altered that much by geographical separation and dispersal. In many respects the answer, perhaps surprisingly, is 'no'.

As we have discussed, most kin ties are not active at a day-to-day level. Some are — a subset of those in people's intimate kin sets — but the majority are not. Most ties are not organized in this way, and most people do not wish them to be. Furthermore, modern technologies have helped render geographical separation less constraining than it was. Telephones and comparatively efficient transport systems have made it easier, especially for those with resources, to see and keep in touch with one another as frequently as they wish. Indeed many kin exchanges do not require a high level of face-to-face contact. Solidarity is expressed in other ways, e.g. through letters, cards, and phone calls. Furthermore, family rituals — birthdays, anniversaries, religious festivals, weddings, and the like — frequently provide people with an opportunity for kinship interaction.

Finally, it is important to note that the effects of increased geographical dispersion cannot easily, or indeed usefully, be understood properly without reference to other changes occurring in society. For example, geographical separation does limit the assistance mothers can give their daughters with child care and other responsibilities. But equally, married women's changed employment patterns, affecting both mother and daughter, of themselves also influence the extent to which such support can be provided. Equally, while geographical mobility can make interaction between siblings less common, it is not this alone which affects the siblings' cohesiveness. The increased diversity fostered by contemporary conditions in the experience, occupation, and life-style of siblings also colour their relationships, a point Rosser and Harris emphasized in their seminal work (1965: 289).

Altered household and family forms

There have been four significant changes in household and family matters that are likely to have had some impact on kin ties, though there is relatively little research concerned specifically with the extent to which they have. These changes are the increased rates of cohabitation, divorce, unmarried mothers, and stepfamilies.

The first of these, higher levels of cohabitation, is probably the least significant in kin terms. For many, cohabitation represents a mode of courtship rather than a long-term form of 'coupledom'. It has become the dominant form of engagement, undertaken as a recognized phase prior to marriage. In such cases the kinship implications are of little consequence. When this is not so, when the couple are living as long-term partners without the intention of marrying, then the main kinship issue is the one alluded to in the story of the journey given at the beginning of Chapter 3. It is the question of when those involved are recognized as kin by others in their partner's family. There will, of course, be variation in this depending in part on whether there are children in the partnership, but also on the time the couple have spent together and their perceived stability. The moral stance taken by different members of the kin group may also have some sway, though as the numbers of people choosing to cohabit increases, this is likely to be of less consequence.

The numbers of births registered to unmarried mothers has increased from less than 10 per cent of all births in the mid-1970s to over 30 per cent by the mid-1990s. Seventeen out of every twenty teenage mothers are unmarried. However, in three-quarters of these births, the father's name is also registered, and in roughly half of them the two parents are cohabiting at the time of registration. While little is known about the longer-term stability of cohabitations where a child is born, the kinship issues are probably little different to those of marriage, especially as a proportion of these cohabitations are likely to result in marriage at some future date. Where there is no cohabitation, and especially where the father's name is not registered, it is more likely that involvement with the father's kin will be quite minimal. Paternal grandparents may attempt to maintain a relationship where paternity is acknowledged, but in many cases this will prove difficult and may come to be defined as 'interfering' by the mother. It would seem that a great deal depends on the character of any continuing relationship between the child's mother and father, which indicates again the importance of the social, as well as the biological and legal, basis of kinship.

Increased levels of divorce raise some very interesting questions about kinship, though there is little British research which examines this specifically. As above, a key issue is the type of relationship the non-residential parent maintains with her or his children and ex-spouse, as this will generally influence the character of the relationships her or his kin maintain with the family. Obviously other factors are of consequence, in particular geographical distance. It must be remembered, though, that up to half the children of divorced parents have less than annual contact with their non-residential parent within a few years of the separation (Lund, 1987). This almost certainly means that the children also lose contact with the grandparents, aunts, and uncles on that side of the family as well.

Overall it would seem that in the great majority of cases there is little contact between divorced people and their ex-spouse's kin. These ties are usually severed in the same way the marriage is after divorce (Hart, 1976; O'Brien, 1987). There are exceptions to this, but these depend upon the strength of the relationship which was developed between particular in-laws prior to the divorce, and also to some degree on the conflict and tension between the couple in the aftermath of the separation. In their examination of kinship ties following divorce, Finch and

Mason (1990) provide details of one female respondent who maintained a very warm and supportive relationship with her ex-mother-in-law which included some care provision. This was an exceptional case, built upon the goodwill and mutual support between the women over a number of years. In other cases, attempts may be made to keep grandparent-grandchildren relationships active, but generally relationships with an ex-spouse's kin over time become more distant.

Increased divorce rates over the last thirty years raise questions about the support that adult children are likely to provide their parents in old age. This is a matter which will be discussed in Chapter 6. Here the issue is the extent to which children will feel any sense of responsibility for parents who 'left' them during childhood. Will they feel higher levels of commitment to their residential parent? Will they be prepared to care for non-residential parents? This is an issue on which it is currently too early to pronounce, as the first generation to experience high divorce levels is only now approaching old age. However, it seems likely that the actual relationship maintained between children and the non-residential parent after the divorce will matter, as will the degree to which there are other carers available. If the parent remarried and had other children, it may be that those children are seen as the more appropriate carers. This is a topic which has received little research attention so far, but one which is of some consequence for current social policy.

Stepfamilies generate a more complex web of relationships than natural families (Robinson and Smith, 1993). This applies both to the ties inside the household and to those outside it. Remarriage may result in a further weakening of the ties maintained with the ex-spouse's kin, but it also creates issues about the relationship between the new spouse's kin and any children from the first marriage. If both new spouses have children from previous marriages and if children are born into the new family, the kinship position can become very complex. For example, to what extent should the new spouse's parents be encouraged to act as grandparents to children from the previous marriage? Is it acceptable for them to behave differently with any 'real' grandchildren they have in the family, either from a first marriage or this new one? To what extent should their relationship depend on that between the children and their grandparents on their non-residential parent's side? As with other stepfamily matters, no social norms or conventions have yet developed over these matters. It is for each individual family to work out for themselves, though it is important to recognize that each of these relationships is part of a wider, and often quite complex, network of kin relationships which will collectively have an influence over each constituent tie.

Ethnic diversity

Since the middle of the century, Britain's black ethnic population has grown as a result of migration from the Caribbean and from parts of Asia. This has led to the population becoming ethnically far more diverse (Mason, 1995). As more people from Commonwealth countries settled in Britain, they brought with them their own cultural beliefs and practices, including different patterns of organizing kin relationships. As with other aspects of culture, these kinship patterns are not static but are responsive to the social and economic conditions under which life is being lived, though for some groups at least they remain closely tied to religious and moral considerations about the meaning of 'family' and about the proper ordering of relationships between the generations.

Migration itself has a bearing on kinship relationships. This is not just in the simple sense that relationships are bound to have a different content when those involved are geographically separated by thousands of miles. More importantly, kinship (and other informal ties) played a significant role in the facilitation of migration to Britain and in residential settlement. That is, when people migrated to Britain, they were often 'sponsored' by kin who were already resident here. These kin provided information about the opportunities that there were, often offered the migrant a home when they first arrived, and helped them find employment. The consequence of this was that frequently, though with some variation, people settled in the same areas as others they knew before migration. Just as Donald in Rosser and Harris's (1965) account of kinship in Wales used his relatives to help him settle in Swansea (see above), so migrants from other countries draw on their already resident kin for support (Ballard, 1994).

In many cases, such kin support continues to be important, both practically and symbolically. In particular, in a racist and hostile 'host' culture in which ethnic minorities are systematically disadvantaged, the support of kin can be crucial in the routine organization of social life. Here, of course, kin do not act alone. Other informal ties with people who share similar backgrounds and experiences are also important in this. Through these links, cultural identities can be sustained and help given in overcoming the dilemmas and contingencies of daily living. Thus, being involved in networks like these with others who share a similar view of the world can provide the individual with a ready source of social, economic, and cultural support (Westwood and Bhachu, 1988; Warrier, 1994).

The cultural aspect of kinship takes on a particular significance in cases of ethnic minorities, especially those whose way of life is devalued by the majority population. The moral code which kinship involves, especially with regard to appropriate ways of caring for older kin and of socializing children, often comes to represent a key difference between majority and minority populations, fuelling a host of racist stereotypes in the process. Yet while traditional ways of ordering life, including kin ties, may be adhered to for the sense of cultural identity this provides, in actuality the 'traditional' ways are routinely modified in response to the economic and social context in which they are enacted (Werbner, 1981; Ballard, 1994). At times, this may involve a more rigid adherence to 'traditional' ways than was common previously, or it may result in new interpretations of old practices. The point is that culture, including kinship, is dynamic. Ideas about how life should be ordered evolve with changing circumstances.

Within Britain's ethnic minorities there is, of course, much diversity in kinship ideology and behaviour. Afro-Caribbean kinship tends to be matrifocal, that is, households are involved more with maternal than paternal kin, partly because of the proportion of female-headed households. However, the degree to which female-headed households are a result of cultural heritage rather than economic disadvantage is an open question. In contrast, among those of South Asian descent, relationships between a husband's kin are often given priority over a wife's, though again the patterns which develop are influenced by social and economic circumstances (Warrier, 1994). So too, some ethnic minorities traditionally emphasize the joint rather than nuclear household, in which two generations live together under the formal authority of the older male. However, while this pattern occurs in some households, it is not found uniformly. Many other households are characterized by a nuclear form, though possibly with some sharing of household activities across different households in the same vicinity (Bhachu, 1985).

Increasingly, families and households are now being formed by second-generation ethnic minorities, that is, by people from ethnic minorities who have spent all their lives in Britain. These people consequently have knowledge of both majority and minority kinship patterns. How this will influence the ordering of their own kin relationships in adult life and, of course, the knowledge they pass on to their children, is a matter of some conjecture and will only be known with time. It seems probable that the patterns which emerge will be affected by the economic position of those involved, their sense of ethnic identity, the degree to which they share a similar heritage to their partners, and the extent to which their social networks are dominated by others from a similar background. Overall, there is likely to be a good deal of variation, with their kinship practices combining some 'traditional' elements with other ones taken from the majority culture (Werbner, 1981).

Conclusion

This chapter started with the question of whether a kinship system exists in contemporary Britain. Some information has been provided in this chapter that in part begins to answer that question. In particular we have noted the comparative unimportance of most secondary kin in people's lives. While some sections of the population are more actively involved than others with secondary kin, and while some secondary kin are important as individuals, overall these people play only a small part in our lives. In the main, that is, we do not feel a strong sense of commitment or obligation to secondary kin and do not rely on them in any significant fashion.

However, we have also left many questions unanswered. For instance, we have said little about the nature of the relationships between primary kin; this is the topic of the next chapter. But nor have we really explored the social (or economic) basis of the solidarity which does exist between kin. We can ask, for example, how important a sense of obligation is in our kin relationships. Is it obligation that determines how we behave? Or should we be thinking in terms of love and altruism? To what extent do we follow 'rules' in our relationships with kin? Or is it better to perceive kinship behaviour as informally negotiated? If so, how and who with? We need to pose such questions if we are to understand better the way in which kinship as a system operates. These are the topics addressed in Chapter 6.

Further reading

As noted above, studies which approach kinship in the way Raymond Firth (1956, 1970) did have not been published recently. However, *Family Obligations and Social Change* (1989) by Janet Finch discusses many of the issues which were raised in this chapter, as well as others to be examined in Chapters 5 and 6. Firth *et al.*'s *Families and their Relatives* (1970) is a very thorough description of kinship patterns which you may find worth browsing. Numerous other family and community studies contain some information on secondary-kin relationships without this being their exclusive focus.

Chapter Five

Primary Kinship

The previous chapter focused on the idea of a kinship system and on the ways in which secondary kin ties are ordered. In this chapter, the focus moves to primary kinship — that is, ties between parents, siblings, and children. As has already been mentioned, in the earlier kinship studies primary kin ties seemed only rarely to break down completely. Most of these ties were relatively active, in nearly all instances continuing in some form or other, though the particular form they took depended on the circumstances of those involved. And in those cases where the ties no longer involved any significant form of personal relationship, where the primary kin concerned said they had little or no contact with one another, accounts were readily offered about how this state of affairs had come about. The breakdown of these relationships, in other words, was seen as undesirable and as something which warranted explanation.

In many respects little has changed here. The moral basis of kinship is still very clearly evident in the ways in which primary kinship ties are understood and, indeed, in the ways in which they are routinely organized. The details of the relationships certainly vary, but there is an overriding moral view that, other things being equal, primary kin should share a commitment to and solidarity with one another. As Parsons (1956) rightly emphasized some years ago, other commitments, and in particular those to spouse/partner and dependent children, are expected to be given priority, but this does not mean that commitments to other primary kin are non-existent (Harris, 1969; Allan, 1985). There are no standard rules about how such solidarity and commitment is most appropriately expressed, but there is an acceptance that these relationships should normally be sustained in a meaningful way.

Yet, as discussed briefly at the end of the last chapter, change has occurred in aspects of domestic and other social organization which does have an impact on the ways in which primary kin ties are constructed. In particular, the dramatic increases there have been in divorce, lone-parent households, and stepfamilies have undoubtedly influenced the character of many primary kin relationships. It will be recalled that in Firth's studies, parental conflict and separation was one of the major causes of primary kin breakdown. These same processes operate twenty-five years on from the publication of Firth's second study, only with greater impact because of the increased incidence of divorce.

Perhaps the main point to emphasize here is that parental separation and divorce is one of the factors which is likely to shape primary kin ties, but only one of them. Like other kinship ties, these relationships do not follow a simple social script. They are normative in the sense that there are strong expectations of continuing commitment, but they are not built upon easily specified, agreed social norms. It is not, in other words, a case of individuals playing out roles which are predefined. Rather, the patterning of the ties is dependent on the circumstances of the individuals involved and the range of different responsibilities they have, including their domestic and familial ones. The pattern these various commitments weave in people's lives, the space within them available for primary kinship ties to occupy, varies quite significantly. And so consequently do the nature and character of the actual relationships which at any given time primary kin construct with each other.

The time dimension is, of course, quite a crucial one here, though in talking about the structure of kinship ties generally this is easy to underplay. Like all relationships, primary kin ones develop over time, in the process generating a distinct history or biography which in turn has an impact on their future patterning. But in addition to understanding relationships in terms of the personal dynamics of their own past, it is important to recognize that the changing circumstances of the individuals involved have a strong influence on the ways in which these relationships are currently constructed. Thus the genealogical parent-child tie is structured quite differently over the life-course, as children move from (childhood) dependence to (adult) independence, and as within adulthood the mesh of the different responsibilities of the two generations alters and changes. In order to examine primary kinship solidarity in more depth, this chapter will focus first on parent-child ties, and then consider sibling relationships.

Parent-child ties

There is no straightforward or uniform way of depicting the detailed relationships which develop between parents and their children in adulthood. As suggested above, too much variation occurs within these ties for this to be possible. Yet it would be equally inappropriate to argue that these relationships do not typically have a common base on which the individuality of the ties is constructed. This common base was perhaps most accurately expressed by David Schneider (1968) when, in discussing the core elements of American kinship, he coined the term 'diffuse enduring solidarity'. In many ways this notion captures especially well the central and overriding quality normatively expected and desired of parent-child bonds.

There are three elements within the concept of 'diffuse enduring solidarity' which make it particularly pertinent for characterizing these ties. First, as we have seen, in the great majority of cases these relationships do endure. They typically last, albeit with different 'contents', over the life-course. Even when there is a degree of animosity and conflict, this is generally not seen as grounds for breaking the relationships. One, or even both, sides may be dissatisfied with the relationship, they may not enjoy their contact, but the relationship still endures, with a recognition of the 'rightness' that this should be so.

Secondly, the commitment which parents and adult children have to each other is diffuse. It is not specific; it is not seen as relevant to narrowly defined areas of social activity. Rather, it is a solidarity which can be activated in a range of ways, dependent upon the particular situation of those involved and the particular needs they have at that time. Within the relationship, each is a resource that can be drawn on as appropriate, though exactly what is seen as appropriate is again a consequence of the biographical development of the relationship and thus of negotiations over time rather than following set or standard cultural conventions.

Thirdly, and stemming from the above, these relationships are typically not ones in which a broad equality of exchange has a high priority. In most of the personal relationships which people construct, including friend ties (discussed more fully in Chapters 7 and 8), equality of exchange does matter. Where one party is seen as too demanding or unwilling to reciprocate the favours and help they have previously received, the tie is likely to become less active. Sometimes tension may become overt and lead to a clear split; in other cases the process of disengagement can be more gradual, with the discontent felt never really being expressed. This, though, is not what routinely happens in parent-adult child relationships. Certainly there can be irritation and tension, indeed sometimes anger, at the demands that are being made, or indeed at too low a perceived level of interest or involvement. Yet this does not usually result in the tie becoming inactive. That is, the implicit calculation of reciprocity appears to play a small part in these relationships. More importantly, there is a strong recognition that exchanges will often be unbalanced. At different stages of the life-course, either side may be demanding and/or receiving a disproportionate amount of support or assistance.

Yet this does not mean that the exchanges within the relationship are without limits. As with any relationship, at a given time there will be a more or less shared definition of what is appropriate or relevant to the tie. Culturally there are two dominant, though somewhat conflicting, principles which give shape to this in parent-adult child relationships. The first of these relates to the degree of independence from parental authority and control which is part of the cultural definition of adulthood. The second, equally powerful, principle is that of familial responsibility, which of course does not end when children become adult. This tension or dialectic between the twin themes of independence and responsibility plays a major part in shaping parent-adult child relationships. This can be recognized in examining different phases of the life-course.

Early adulthood

Consider first the phase of early adulthood. The process of adolescence can generally be understood as one in which young individuals gradually assert their independence and move away from parental control and domination of their lives. At this stage there is still a strong sense of parental responsibility, but this is accompanied by an apparently declining influence and a conscious desire by the younger generation to construct a separate social identity and a social life outside the family. The break from parental control is most marked when the child leaves home and becomes more fully domestically and financially independent. In the past this movement from the parental home typically took different paths for men and women. Men often left home for education, training, or work reasons, while women were far more likely to make this break on marriage.

However, over the last generation there have been significant changes in these patterns, as Gill Jones's (1995) research has shown. First, far more women are entering higher education than was the case twenty years ago. Secondly, patterns of family formation have altered quite dramatically. Not only has the average age of first marriage for females risen from 21 in the late 1960s and early 1970s to 25 by the mid-1990s, but also most people are now cohabiting for a period prior to marriage. Unemployment and changes in social security rules have also had an impact on the extent to which some young people have the resources to live independently (Allatt and Yeandle, 1991; Wallace, 1987; Hutson and Jenkins, 1989).

Jones (1995) also shows how the process of leaving home is often quite drawn out. For example, many young people attending university continue to regard the parental home as 'home'. They go back in vacations, though for less frequent or lengthy periods as their studies progress. Similarly, some people who leave home for employment reasons or to cohabit may return at some later time when, say, they obtain different work or when their relationship ends. Thus the break with the parental home is more gradual and more subtle than is usually assumed. Indeed, independence itself should not be regarded as an either/or state; it evidently contains various dimensions which do not always operate in unison. Students may, for example, no longer live at home, but they may continue to receive financial support. People living in their own flats or in shared houses may still return at weekends for meals or to get washing done.

As mentioned in Chapter 3, Leonard (1980) showed in her analysis of engaged couples how mothers in particular helped their daughters, and to a lesser extent their sons, to prepare for setting up their own homes. In the main they did this by subsidizing the costs of living at home, for example by not taking much money for rent or board, and through buying a range of small presents for 'the bottom drawer', i.e. for use in the new household after the marriage. Leonard pointed out that these processes involved an implicit system of exchange, and not just the expression of love and care. What was being exchanged was material assistance in return for a continued involvement by the parents in the children's lives, at a time of major structural change within the household. Leonard argues that by giving, apparently freely and generously, the mother helped ensure that the relationship between parent and child did not dissipate. It was a way of smoothing this change and of sustaining the right to continue to be involved in the child's life.

Equally it can be recognized that similar processes, although in different guises, continue to operate now in the changed circumstances under which young adults express their independence. The financial contribution parents give to many students is one element of it. Of course, the more this is seen as a right which children have, rather than a gift which parents bestow, the less it can work in this fashion. Similarly, the encouragement of children to bring dirty washing home, or to come home for some 'real' cooking and 'proper' food, is a way of ensuring a level of commitment from the younger generation. The comments and jokes which might be made about this — 'Oh, we only ever see you when you want your washing done/when you're fed up with take-aways/when you need some money' — should be read as ways of ensuring that children realize that their parents are, in Leonard's terms, 'spoiling' them. Here there is an interesting balancing act occurring. On the one hand, parents do appear typically to engage in such 'spoiling'; on the other, a picture is presented of them as being generous and going beyond the bounds of what can rightfully, or normatively, be expected. It is because of this that the process works in the way Leonard describes.

Marriage and settling down

Already within this more independent relationship are the elements which will colour the relationship in the future. Typically the next phase of adulthood for the child is one of 'settling down', with marriage, career construction, and child-rearing dominating for many. In this phase, as before, the exchanges which occur between parent and adult child reflect the dialectic between the ideology of independence of nuclear families and the continuing commitments of primary kin, but do so within the context of the changed circumstances under which their lives are lived. Certainly there is continuing involvement of parents and their adult children in each other's lives. Each has a degree of commitment to the other's welfare and each generally recognizes the other's right to know about key aspects of their life, especially concerning major events or changes and domestic/familial aspects. How close these ties are in emotional terms, how much confiding there is, appears to vary a good deal, with gender, class, and the character of the relationship in earlier stages appearing to be important influences (O'Connor, 1990).

Thus there is a mutual recognition of the legitimacy and appropriateness of each being involved at some level in the other's life: parents and adult children should keep each other informed of what, in general, is happening to them. But while this is accepted, it is also generally accepted that too much influence — or in cultural terms, interference — is inappropriate. The difficulty lies in specifying what precisely counts as interference, as this varies widely. In the older studies mentioned in Chapter 3, there were clear class and gender differences in the level of involvement which was seen as normal. In the so-called traditional working-class localities, mothers and their daughters were portrayed as leading interdependent lives of a form that many middle-class women would have rejected. Men generally were less involved in their parents'/adult children's lives, taking an interest but not sharing activities to the same degree.

With hindsight, the strength of these findings can be queried, partly because these traditional localities were probably more diverse than they then appeared, but also because the studies were deliberately reacting to arguments that with modernity, kinship solidarity had become of little consequence. Nonetheless, the general drift of their conclusions continues to receive support. The tie between working-class women with young children and their mothers does still routinely appear to be stronger than other parent-adult child ties. Their mothers are a resource which those at this phase of life draw on quite regularly to help them with the daily tasks they face in bringing up children and running a household. A shared expertise in domestic and child-care matters often fosters this bond, though O'Connor (1990) is right to introduce a note of caution to overly romantic accounts of this relationship. Equally, while middle-class women, with their different career patterns, different geographical mobility, and different resources, are usually not so highly involved with their mothers, they do tend to be incorporated more in parent-adult child ties than men are with either their parents or their children.

Indeed, gender seems to be an important element in the maintenance of these relationships more generally. The issue here is not which particular relationships are most active, but rather who it is who is seen as most responsible for servicing these ties. Despite some resistance, it is wives who give more attention to the set of kin relationships than men (Rosser and Harris, 1965; Rosenthal, 1985; di Leonardo, 1987; Cotterill, 1994). They are usually the ones to remember birthdays, buy cards and presents; they are the ones who arrange visits; one suspects they are the ones who keep conversations between these kin flowing and who work hardest at managing them. The old saying 'A son's a son till he gets him a wife; a daughter's a daughter the rest of her life' seems apt, with the proviso that once he gets him a wife, the wife often seems

---

Activity 5.1 A Kin Diary

Keep a diary for a week. Note every time any kinsperson outside your household is mentioned. Who starts the conversation? Who is expected to be active? Who expresses most concern? See if there is a gender difference in this.

---

to be handed much of the kinship orchestration. It appears to be seen as part of the domestic-servicer role which still tends to dominate women's social location and identity.

The idea of some kin acting as intermediaries highlights the point that kinship ties, of whatever form, are not just matters of the personal tie in question. The significance of people acting as intermediaries is that by doing so they help sustain the relationship between others. This issue has more general applicability. We have already referred to the importance of seeing kinship as a network of individuals linked to one another through socially active genealogical ties. This notion of kinship as a network is of consequence in understanding parent-adult child ties, for often the presence of other kin influences the path these relationships take (Harris, 1990).

Consider for example the impact that marriage or other more-or-less permanent partnerships can have on these ties. As suggested above, the setting up of a home with another person, inside or outside of marriage, can symbolize the breaking from the parental family as much as any other process. So too the commitment there is to the new partner is potentially a source of distance between parent and child. However, whether or not it acts like this is likely to be influenced quite heavily by the relationships which are developed between the partner and the parents. In other words, what is likely to matter here is not just the individual tie, with its history of co-operation and conflict, but also the way this is mediated by the relationship between these others. Where this is positive, it is likely to strengthen the link between parent and adult child; where there is ill-feeling or dislike, the relationship between the parents and their child is likely to become more strained, even if it remains active.

Similarly, and perhaps more noticeably, when grandchildren are born the relationship between grandparent and parent is given a new basis. They share a commitment to the (grand)child, with parents generally recognizing the legitimacy of involving the grandparents in the new child's life. Of course arguments can develop over appropriate child-care methods, over 'spoiling' and too much interference, but more often the presence of the child gives a new 'family' focus to the relationship between the adult generations (Cunningham-Burley, 1985). Whereas previously there may have been relatively little, aside from the generalized enduring solidarity, maintaining the link, now the new focus of the (grand)child provides an obvious common theme. The continued involvement of grandparents and grandchildren as the latter grow up provides an important framing for the parent-adult child relationship. It is in such ways that kinship needs to be understood as a network of ties rather than as a series of unconnected individual relationships.

Just as Leonard's (1980) mothers 'spoiled' their children when the latter were about to get married and leave home, so the same process operates with grandchildren. Not only do grandparents frequently buy small gifts for their grandchildren — sweets, clothes, toys, etc. — but they also help out the parents with the costs of child-rearing. They may on occasion, for example, buy them bikes or pay for holidays or contribute to the costs of private schooling. Clearly the extent to which they do help in such ways depends on their own resources and class position as well as that of their adult children. But no matter what the form of gift-giving, the process is typically equivalent to that discussed earlier in the summary of Bell's (1968) and Leonard's (1980) studies. That is, the giving of gifts is a way of maintaining a legitimate right to be involved in the grandchildren's and the children's lives. This does not mean that such gifts are not given through love, but it does mean that there are social consequences to such giving whose power comes from their not being vocalized.

Moreover, the giving of gifts to and for grandchildren is a way of maintaining involvement without undermining the principle of independence, at a time of life-course inequality in resources (Bell, 1968). Put simply, the time when children are young is the time when many parents experience their greatest poverty. Often only one parent is employed; for those in owner-occupation mortgage repayments are likely to be high; and new child-rearing costs have to be met. For grandparents, on the other hand, this is likely to be a phase of life in which they are relatively prosperous. With two incomes coming in, mortgages repaid or reduced by inflation, and children no longer dependent, they are likely to have more money to spend freely than at other life stages. In addition, some will by then have inherited money from their own (now deceased) parents. Thus the first generation may have resources to spare when the second generation is most in need. To give directly here may undermine independence, but to give it as gifts to or for grand-children does not. In this guise it is likely to prove more acceptable, though the consequence of freeing up the parents' limited resources is the same. The 'cost' (or 'benefit' depending on one's viewpoint) is that the parent-adult child tie is further cemented. Generally here, to accept gifts is to accept the legitimacy of the giver's involvement, without reacting to it as interference, though the line remains a fine one.

At times, adult children can come to rely more heavily than usual on support and assistance from parents as a result of changes in their own situation. For example, when a child experiences unemployment, parents may well attempt to help the household by making financial and other material resources available. Because of the difficulties of threatening independence, especially at a time when self-image may already be under threat through lack of employment, such assistance may need to be 'dressed up' so as not to appear as charity. Again, offering to pay for clothes, gifts, or treats for grandchildren is often an acceptable way of effecting a transfer of resources across the generations (Binns and Mars, 1984; McKee, 1987; Gallie *et al.* eds., 1994). Similarly, after separation and divorce, daughters and/or sons sometimes return to the parental home to live, especially if there are (grand)children who need a home. Such arrangements are rarely thought of as ideal or more than temporary. But they do indicate the enduring solidarity that parents have with their children (and grand-children). While conflict can result from overcrowding and the lack of autonomy which the adult child may experience, returning to the parental home at this time of major emotional and material change can offer a degree of security and comfort.

Old age

As parents age, their relationships with their children tend to be modified, though the process is usually a gradual one. Illness, infirmity, and widowhood can change the nature of the relative dependencies, though these events usually happen in later rather than earlier old age. Given demographic patterns, the children of those who are 75 and over are themselves often at or near the grandparental phase of the life-course. Their domestic responsibilities are altering as their own children leave home. Here it is important, as before, to recognize that the current relationship between parents and their adult children has a (now long) history which will influence, though not determine, the content and character of these relationships as parents reach a life stage in which potentially they may need more support.

But of course most elderly parents do not need much active care. They are quite capable of managing for themselves as they have done throughout the life-course. They may be that much frailer and find some activities harder to complete, but they generally have no desire to be seen as dependent on their children. Similar issues arise here as when children become adult. Elderly people do not wish to give up their independence or rely in a clearly unreciprocated fashion on others. Thus at this phase of the life-course, as elderly parents find some tasks more difficult, children often need to develop relatively subtle ways of providing support without this undermining the self-image of the parent. Gradually more visits may be made, and more help with shopping, household repairs, and other practical tasks given in ways which are found acceptable. In the best Goffman (1959) tradition, connivance is quite likely from both sides in this to ensure that there is no explicit expression of increasing dependence.

However, there are limits to this. If elderly parents become infirm then typically at least one child will become more involved in providing a level of support. Indeed, there are suggestions in the research literature on caring that this happens even if the parent is not particularly well-liked or if the previous relationship has been marked by tension (Ungerson, 1987). It is as yet unclear how the spread of divorce and remarriage will influence these patterns, especially given the comparative lack of contact there often is between children and their non-residential parent. However, the diffuse enduring solidarity characteristic of parent-adult child relationships ensures that in the main children are concerned about their parents' welfare, especially if they appear to be 'failing to thrive' when living independently. Contrary to popular stereotypes to the contrary, adult children play a major role in helping parents to sustain an independent life-style for as long as possible. (See Chapter 6 for a fuller discussion of these issues.)

Siblings

Schneider's (1968) concept of 'diffuse enduring solidarity' also applies to sibling relationships. There is generally a lower level of participation and involvement in these relationships than with parent-adult child ones, and also a lesser sense of responsibility. Nonetheless the ties typically endure and do usually involve a generalized concern for the other's welfare. Within this, there is a wide range of actual behaviour, some siblings regarding one another as 'best friends', whilst others are far less active. Generalizing about these ties is also more difficult, as the biography and developmental conditions of these ties are more variable. For example, the numbers of siblings and their distribution in terms of age and gender can all have an impact on the actual ties which develop between any pair. Thus, in larger families the age gap between youngest and oldest sibling may mean that there is rather little contact between them. Similarly, the picture gets complex when the different living arrangements and interactional patterns of stepbrothers and stepsisters are considered.

In addition, studies which focus on adult siblings are quite rare, especially in Britain. However, the complex interplay of co-operation and conflict which often seems to characterize sibling relationships in childhood and adolescence appears to be largely dissipated when the siblings no longer live together. Given the comparatively petty nature of many of these sibling squabbles, their basis in shared living, and the limited exchange content of most sibling relationships in adulthood, it is not surprising that few people appear to have strongly negative relationships with adult siblings. Most of these ties are managed without high levels of tension becoming manifest, although occasionally conflict can re-emerge over issues to do with the provision of parental care or the distribution of property after parental death.

As with parent-adult child ties, adult sibling relationships are influenced by the network of other relationships in which they are embedded. Two issues are particularly relevant here. First, parents generally play an important part in sustaining sibling relationships. In part they do this through facilitating and arranging interaction. So, for example, if a sibling who lives some distance away comes to visit parents, then other, more local siblings are likely to see them then too. They will be invited over or visited at some time during the stay. But parents also help sustain sibling ties by acting as a communication channel. As already mentioned, when kin meet, a major topic of conversation is the kinship group itself. Thus, news and information about each sibling's activities and plans are routinely passed on to other siblings through the parents, who act like a switchboard. When parents die, some sibling ties become less active because of the absence of this mediation in the relationship.

Second, sibling relationships are shaped by the ways in which their partners/spouses get along together. Where this relationship is a positive one, where the siblings-in-law like one another and share interests in common, then the sibling tie itself is likely to be cemented further. For instance, visits are more likely to be arranged, different social activities shared, and holidays taken together. Where the siblings-in-law do not feel comfortable with each other, contact is usually maintained, especially through the intercession of parents, but the relationship will normally involve less interaction and have a lower exchange basis.

Some sibling relationships are particularly close ones. The siblings regard each other as friends in a full sense, sometimes describing the other as being their 'best friend', and share a wide range of activities together. In a small-scale piece of research conducted in the early 1970s, it was noticeable that working-class respondents frequently described a particular sibling — nearly always the one of the same gender closest in age to them — as their closest friend (Allan, 1979). They met with this sibling very regularly and often undertook all their main social activities together. As above, it was significant in this that the siblings' spouses also had close ties, so that it was generally two couples acting together rather than just two siblings. This pattern seems less common amongst middle-class people, though there may also be a gender difference here, with women confiding more to a particular sister than brothers do.

It could also be that age has a bearing on closer solidarity between particular siblings, particularly for sisters. Dorothy Jerrome (1981), for example, has suggested that some sibling ties become closer and more participative in later life, especially if the siblings have remained single or have been recently widowed. Here decreasing social participation, through changing marital, domestic, and employment roles, at a time when the encroachment of infirmity makes independence riskier and more difficult to manage, is likely to heighten the need for companionship within the home. Even though siblings may not have been particularly close in previous life stages, the enduring solidarity between them, together with their shared history and the detailed knowledge they have of one another's past, appears to make them appropriate and suitable living companions at this time. The tensions and niggles of the past may sometimes surface, but the basis of solidarity makes the relationship in this new guise manageable.

Conclusion

This chapter has focused on primary kin and discussed the character of the solidarity which typically exists between these kin. There are, of course, variations in the relationships primary kin maintain with one another. The detailed content of any relationship is affected by a wide range of factors, including the history of that particular tie. However, there do seem to be common strands within most primary kin ties, appropriately, albeit loosely, captured by Schneider's concept of 'diffuse enduring solidarity'. How that solidarity is expressed, what forms of support are given, what is considered relevant to the tie varies over the life-course depending on each party's circumstances.

What has not been discussed in this chapter are the processes by which that solidarity is sustained. This is the theme of the next chapter, which examines the role that obligation and normative sanction plays in kinship ties, especially with respect to elderly kin in need of some support. Drawing on the work of Finch and Mason (Finch, 1989; Finch and Mason, 1993), it will examine how kinship behaviour is negotiated over time, either explicitly or implicitly, and briefly consider the impact which material and economic concerns have on this. In the process, it will make reference to the ways in which the personal and moral identities created through earlier kinship interaction have consequences for later kinship behaviour.

Further reading

Janet Finch's *Family Obligations and Social Change* (1989) addresses many of the issues covered in this chapter. It also informs the discussion in Chapter 6. Other books contain material relevant to parts of Chapter 5, but generally not as their main theme. For example, Gill Jones's *Leaving Home* (1995) provides a good discussion of early adulthood; *Desh Pardesh: The South Asian Presence in Britain* (1994), edited by Roger Ballard, contains many chapters in which kinship issues are examined; while in *Friendly Relations?* (1994) Pamela Cotterill concentrates on ties between the mother-in-law and daughter-in-law, but in the process discusses the character of other primary kin relationships.

Chapter Six

Kinship, Obligation, and Care

Previous chapters have examined the nature of kinship solidarity in modern Britain and some of the variations that are found in it. This chapter continues with that theme, though in doing so approaches the matter from a slightly different angle. In order to understand more fully the character of kinship solidarity, we will focus on a particular phase of the life-course — old age — and examine how solidarity between kin is expressed at this time. It will be concerned especially with the sense of responsibility people feel towards elderly kin as they become more dependent and in need of forms of personal care. The ways in which this transformation towards greater dependency is managed highlights many important features within contemporary kinship. Before looking more closely at these issues, however, it is necessary to discuss the situation of elderly people in the population more generally so as to provide a framework for understanding patterns of kinship behaviour.

Elderly people and the need for care

The number of elderly people in Great Britain has increased quite dramatically over the course of the twentieth century. This is shown in Table 6.1. As can be seen from this, at the turn of the century there were slightly over half a million people over the age of 75, including some 60,000 over the age of 85. By 1991, the numbers over 75 had increased almost eight-fold to over 4 million, while the number of people aged 85 or over had increased by a factor of fifteen to over 900,000.

While there is a correlation between age and infirmity, in particular for those aged over 85, it is a far from perfect one. It is consequently important to recognize that the great majority of elderly people live

Table 6.1 Elderly People in the British Population, 1901 and 1991 (thousands)

	1901			1991		
	Men	Women	Total	Men	Women	Total
65+	784	1,025	1,809	3,637	5,468	9,105
75+	219	312	531	1,365	2,673	4,038
85+	23	38	61	214	687	901

Source: Annual Abstract of Statistics, 1995.

quite independently without any need for others to provide them with personal care. Moreover, that independence is highly valued. The ability to make one's own decisions and take care of one's own needs is a central feature of adult life and a symbol of social competence. Few people seek to become dependent on others or welcome this when it occurs.

One problem in estimating how many older people are in need of care and support from others lies in defining what counts as 'in need of support'. A key issue here is that virtually everyone receives support and care from others, irrespective of their age or infirmity. People living in the same household, for example, provide all sorts of support for one another and help each other in a variety of tasks. So too kin, friends, and others living in different households routinely provide small favours for one another and help each other cope with whatever issues and problems arise in daily living. This is entirely normal and unexceptional, part and parcel of the reciprocal exchanges which lie at the heart of many personal relationships. But the key point about them is that they are reciprocal. There is not usually a one-way flow of support.

However, as people become more infirm, so they are less able to reciprocate the support they receive. In such a way, they gradually or otherwise become increasingly dependent. The General Household Survey — a large-scale national survey of the circumstances of a randomly selected set of households and the individuals living in them — provides some of the most reliable data on infirmity and support needs. It uses a simple measure of dependency based on whether individuals can carry out certain key activities for themselves. These include washing and bathing, walking outside their house, and climbing stairs. For each of six measures, people are assigned a score of 0, 1, or 2 depending on whether they can do these tasks unaided, with the help of another person, or not at all. Thus the most infirm — those who cannot do any of these tasks for themselves — score 12, while those who need no support at all score 0. Conventionally, those with a score of 6 or more are defined as severely infirm (Arber and Ginn, 1992).

Using this measure, Arber and Ginn (1992) have shown that some 20 per cent of those aged 75 or over, and nearly 40 per cent of those aged 85 or more, fall within this category. As Table 6.2 indicates, many of these people live in households with others, usually spouses, sometimes siblings, sometimes unmarried sons or daughters. A small number live with the children and children-in-law together with any (grand)-children the latter have. Where there is co-residence, much of the support the elderly person requires will be provided by the others in the household, though not necessarily on an equal basis. However, nearly two-fifths of elderly people with severe infirmity live alone. The great majority of these people are female, largely as a consequence of demographic factors, in particular the fact that men marry at an older age and have a shorter life expectancy.

Table 6.2 Living Circumstances of Elderly People with Severe Disability (%)

	Men	Women	All
Lives alone	21	43	38
Lives in own household with spouse	63	30	38
Lives in own household with others	8	12	11
Lives in adult child's household	6	12	10
Lives in someone else's household	2	3	3

Source: Arber and Ginn, 1992.

Sometimes the fact that so many people in need of support live alone is taken as a sign that families are failing to provide the care that they should. Certainly there are some dependent elderly people who receive very little support in managing their lives from children or other relatives. And, of course, there are others who never had children or who now have none living. But there are many others who do live alone, and who are able to maintain this prime symbol of independence, precisely because their families, together with health and social services agencies, are active in providing them with support as necessary to enable them to do so.

Although the need for support can arise quite suddenly, for example as the result of a major stroke, quite often the move towards greater dependency on others is a gradual process. Indeed, informal care and support can best be viewed as a continuum. At one end is the need for systematic, long-term, and extensive support in order that the elderly person can survive. But at the other end, the help and services provided may not even be seen, perhaps especially by the recipient, as 'support'. Instead it will be defined as an unremarkable part of family life, an element within the routine and continuing exchanges of assistance which close kin give one another (Finch and Mason, 1993). However, as physical or mental infirmity increases, then the support that is required also gradually grows. What starts off as relatively low-level and routine can, over time, become far more onerous. Slowly it ceases to be part of the normal give and take of familial exchange and instead becomes a far more marked one-way flow of support (Allan, 1986).

Who cares?

A key question which arises here, and one which is of major consequence for public policy given the current emphasis on the role of informal relationships in care provision, concerns who it is who actually does provide care — or 'tending' in Parker's (1981) phrase — if it is needed. Indeed, more generally, are there 'rules' about who has responsibility for providing support to elderly people as they become increasingly frail? Are there 'rules' within the kinship system that specify which kin should be most heavily involved? Are decisions reached by the wider kin group as a whole or do individual kin act alone? Are there 'norms' over how caring is divided between different kin? What role can friends and other non-kin associates be expected to play?

In effect, what these questions are asking is this: 'Is there an agreed set of rules or principles covering the care obligations which people have towards their infirm elderly relatives?' This in turn, though, as Janet Finch and Jennifer Mason's recent analyses have shown (Finch, 1989; Finch and Mason, 1993), embraces two levels of question. First, in terms of publicly expressed norms and ideologies of kinship, do people have a sense of obligation towards those of their elderly kin who need higher levels of support? Do they consider it legitimate that their time, effort, and other resources be used in providing such care? And if so, which kin have what degree of obligation? Second, if there is a sense of obligation, how does this get expressed in practice? How is it affected by other obligations which people also see as legitimate? In what ways, and with what consequences, can people 'ignore' or override their apparent obligations to infirm, elderly kin?

Qureshi and Walker (1989) conducted research in Sheffield to uncover the circumstances under which relatives are likely to provide
elderly people with support. In their study, they interviewed a sample of
306 people over the age of 75, together with 57 of the carers these people
identified. From the comments these respondents made, they were able
to construct a broad hierarchical model of kinship responsibility. The
attraction of the model is that while simple, it is also intelligible at a
'common-sense' level. It is as most people would expect, thereby indicating its accuracy as a reflection of people's kinship assumptions.

Figure 6.1 Qureshi and Walker's Model of Kinship Responsibility
(1989: 126)

1. Spouse
2. Relative in lifelong joint household
3. Daughter
4. Daughter-in-law
5. Son
6. Other relative
7. Non-relative

Moreover, some 80 per cent of the cases where there was a single
principal carer in Qureshi and Walker's study matched the predictions
arising from the model. That is, for example, when there was someone
else living in the same household as the elderly, infirm person, in the
great majority of cases they were the ones who acted as primary carer.
Similarly, when the elderly person had a daughter living nearby but no
one in the same household, the daughter was likely to be the chief carer.

There are a number of points which arise from this model which
warrant further discussion. First, it is worth emphasizing the role of
spouses in providing care. In recent years, the debates about caring
have often stressed the very high cost that daughters, daughters-in-law,
and in some instances other female relatives have borne in providing
care for severely infirm elderly relatives. This was quite appropriate
given the degree to which support was commonly viewed by the State
and others as 'family care', with the implicit assumption that such care
was both ungendered and shared equally between all family members.
However, this emphasis on second-generation female carers did tend to
disguise the extent to which elderly care was provided by other elderly
people, in particular spouses. While many wives provide support for
their infirm husbands, in a significant number of cases the care is pro-

vided by husbands. Other people may help them in this, especially daughters or daughters-in-law living locally; and it may be that husbands often approach their caring tasks in a different way to wives (Ungerson, 1987). Nonetheless, where a wife is incapacitated in old age, husbands appear typically to undertake much of the routine tending work (Arber and Gilbert, 1989).

Second, the household is clearly an important unit within the provision of care and support, in old age as much as in other life phases. Those sharing a household expect to provide a range of services for one another. When higher levels of care are required, it is usually another person in the household, and in particular a spouse, who provides it rather than someone from outside that domestic unit. In some cases the elderly person will have moved in with a daughter or son specifically because they are now in need of greater support. In other cases though, the person living in the household, usually an adult son or daughter, will have lived there most of their lives. Some of these people of course may themselves be disabled in some way and have been receiving care from their parent(s) throughout their lives. The need to provide care now for an elderly parent may create an extremely difficult situation.

Third, as implied above, if there is no one in the household to provide the support required, the next 'level' of carer is typically a daughter, followed by a daughter-in-law. The research literature referred to above which has been built up since the early 1980s demonstrates very clearly that daughters and daughters-in-law carry a far heavier burden of caring than sons (or sons-in-law). The most graphic illustration of this, although based on a small-scale study which cannot claim to be representative, was Nissel and Bonnerjea's (1982) finding that women in households in which there lived an infirm elderly parent spent on average two to three hours per day providing active care, whilst their husbands spent on average eight minutes. (See also Briggs and Oliver, 1985; Finch and Groves, 1983; Lewis and Meredith, 1988.)

Fourth, research knowledge on the support primary carers receive from others is quite sparse. Generally it seems that ideas of 'networks of carers' (e.g. Barclay Report, 1982) co-ordinating effort and assisting one another in providing consolidated care do not reflect the reality most carers experience. Usually the primary carer seems to receive comparatively little support from others, especially others outside the household, in their caring work (Allan, 1986). The reasons for this are complex and will be discussed further below. However, it is worth noting here that women appear more likely than men to provide 'back-up' support to other primary carers in the practical tasks of tending. For example, typically it is daughters who seem to be more involved in helping one parent care for their infirm spouse when both are alive, and it is sisters (or sisters-in-law) who are more likely to assist one another in looking after an infirm parent still living independently (Finch and Groves, 1983; Lewis and Meredith, 1988).

Finally, note that non-kin rank last in Qureshi and Walker's hierarchy. Only rarely do such people provide high levels of support if they do not live in the same household. They may provide support for older people when there are no kin involved, but providing care is seen predominantly as a family matter. Thus while neighbours and friends may provide practical help, and occasionally more personal tending, for elderly people who are no longer able to manage so well, they tend to be less forthcoming when family members are regularly involved in providing support. That is, because care, and especially more personal care, is seen as a family issue, non-kin often seem to be hesitant about involving themselves once kin take on a caring role. In this, notions of family privacy, of minding one's own business and of not 'interfering', seem important in limiting the involvement of neighbours and other non-kin. Again, this raises questions about the viability of care policies which assume a network of carers can be mobilized relatively easily so as to limit the burden of support a single primary carer carries (Allan, 1991).

Obligation or negotiation?

When people talk about providing support for elderly relatives, especially their parents, they often use the language of obligation and responsibility. They argue, for example, that after all that their parents have done for them over the years, they have a duty to care for them in old age. Or they say they owe it to their parents to help them, as infirmity makes their lives more difficult. The question this poses is whether decisions about the provision of support for specific relatives are based simply on an overriding sense of obligation and duty, or whether other factors influence these decisions. If so, what are these other factors? And how do they relate to the feelings of obligation which people draw on to explain their actions?

The British research which addresses these types of question most fully is that conducted by Janet Finch and Jennifer Mason in the late 1980s and early 1990s (Finch, 1989; Finch and Mason, 1993). This two-pronged research, involving both a large structured survey and in-depth interviews with a smaller sample of respondents, set out to analyse the nature of contemporary kinship responsibility. In particular, it asked whether there was any consensus over what kin should do for one another and how it is that particular individuals end up providing support. A crucial distinction Finch and Mason make is between the public statements individuals make and their more private actions, between public expressions of kinship morality and the ways people actually behave towards their kin. These two aspects of kinship — ideology and behaviour — are, of course, likely to be linked. They are not discrete from one another, but nor, importantly, can actions simply be 'read off' from stated beliefs.

A first issue to resolve is whether in fact there is consensus over kinship beliefs. We saw from Qureshi and Walker's (1989) research that there is broad agreement on the ordering of responsibility. But do people generally agree on the specifics of what kin should do for one another in given circumstances? Do they put the same limits on what it is reasonable to expect kin to do? The first part of Finch and Mason's study was designed to shed light on these types of issue. In this part they asked almost a thousand people about their attitudes towards helping kin. As well as asking people for their responses to individual questions and statements about kinship, Finch and Mason also tapped their respondents' kinship beliefs through the responses given to a series of hypothetical vignettes which were specially constructed for the research. In these a kinship story slowly unfolded, with respondents being able to give their views at different stages throughout the telling of the vignette (Finch, 1987). This approach has the advantage of situating the questions in a context in a way which more general questions about kinship obligation cannot do. An example of one of their vignettes is given below (Figures 6.2 and 6.3).

Finch and Mason found rather little agreement in the responses people gave to the questions they asked about kinship dilemmas. Of the 69 main kinship issues included in the survey, only about half revealed a high degree of consensus. For example, nearly 80 per cent of the respondents agreed that a 19-year-old girl who has a baby should return to her parents' home after she splits up with her boyfriend and can no longer go on living in his home. Similarly, only 3 per cent felt it would be appropriate for relatives to lend money so that parents who could otherwise not afford it could send their two children to private schools. On the other hand, there was disagreement, for example, over whether there were any circumstances in which it would be acceptable to borrow money from relatives, with half the respondents saying 'yes' and half saying 'no' (Finch and Mason, 1993: 198–205).

Similarly the responses to the following (shortened) vignette were

---

Figure 6.2 Kinship Vignette: Early Stage

Jim and Margaret Robinson are a married couple in their early forties. Jim's parents, who live several hundred miles away, have had a serious car accident, and they need long-term daily care and help. Jim is their only son. He and his wife work for the Electricity Board and both could get transfers so that they could work near his parents. What should Jim and Margaret do?

  Move to live near Jim's parents
  Have Jim's parents move to live near them
  Give money to help pay for daily care
  Let them make their own arrangements

---

less than uniform. As you read it, think what answers you would have given at each stage. A third of the survey respondents said Jim and Margaret should move; a quarter said that his parents should come to live with them; and a further quarter thought Jim and Margaret should provide money for care. Thus, while there appears to be agreement that Jim and Margaret have a responsibility to do something in this situation, there is no consensus over what it should be.

There were a series of further stages in this vignette (see Finch, 1987). The last one was as follows:

Figure 6.3 Kinship Vignette: Final Stage

Jim and Margaret do decide to go and live near Jim's parents. A year later Jim's mother dies, and his father's condition gets worse so that he needs full-time care.
  Should Jim or Margaret give up their job to take care of Jim's father?

  Yes, Jim should give up his job
  Yes, Margaret should give up her job
  No, neither should give up their job
  Don't know/Depends

On this issue there was much more agreement, though it was not total. Only 22 per cent of the respondents felt that either Jim or Margaret should give up their jobs, with 64 per cent saying that neither should (Finch and Mason, 1993: 63).

What Finch and Mason argue from this part of their study is that there is little agreement about the 'rules' or public norms of kinship. Different people express different notions of what is right and 'proper', of what people can and cannot expect of their various relatives. In some respects, Finch and Mason's argument here is at odds with what has been written in earlier chapters of this book, in part because they tend not to make discriminations between different categories of kin in their work. Thus their questions are often posed in terms of whether 'relatives' should provide support rather than asking specifically whether parents, cousins, siblings, or whatever should provide support. If they had done this more, they may well have found greater agreement about the boundaries of obligation of secondary kinship in particular. Equally, though, their research is especially useful for showing that at the level of *what* should be done — as distinct from whether *anything* should be done — there really is little consensus.

Why should this be so? Is it the case simply that there is no agreement over kinship responsibilities, or is it that a different set of questions needs to be asked? Finch and Mason are very clear on their answer to this, arguing that kinship behaviour cannot be understood properly from a perspective that sees it solely as rule-following. Rather than just applying a set of agreed norms or standards to kinship issues, what they suggest occurs is a process of *negotiation* over the ways in which the sense of responsibility people have for specific kin is activated in different circumstances.

This notion of negotiation is important but also complex. It does not mean that on each occasion in which a kinship decision is made, the kin involved sit down and explicitly negotiate with one another. Rather, it refers to the ways in which kinship responsibilities are worked out over time between different kin, often without any of the people involved recognizing overtly that 'negotiations' are actually taking place. That is, while on occasion negotiations may be explicit, frequently they are implicit, developing in ways which are dependent on the specific context in question, the 'kinship biographies' of the different people involved, and the various other obligations and responsibilities they have. Indeed, Finch and Mason suggest that explicit and implicit negotiations represent two ends of a spectrum rather than alternatives. Most negotiations involve some elements of both in different combinations (ibid. 64).

Finch and Mason distinguish between three forms of negotiating: open discussions; clear intentions; and non-decisions. Open discussions are those cases where two or more kin openly discuss some kinship issue in order to resolve it. In some cases these are described as 'family conferences', though this does not mean that all the relatives potentially involved are party to them. In Finch and Mason's in-depth interviews, people reported having 'open discussions' over a wide range of issues, including the provision of care for infirm parents. While the idea of 'open discussions' makes the process of kinship responsibility seem quite overt and rational, in reality it is rarely this straightforward. Not only are some people not included, but more importantly the discussions which occur take place within a broader context of knowledge about and commitment to existing relationships. Thus the decisions reached are framed by a tacit understanding of what is actually feasible, based on the biographies of those involved rather than being wholly open to discussion (ibid. 65–71).

'Clear intentions' refer to cases where people have individually decided on a course of action and then implicitly, rather than through open discussion, conveyed that decision to the other kin involved. In a number of instances the main reason for this was to ensure that the balance between independence and dependence was not disrupted. Thus, someone may decide to assist an elderly and infirm parent by, for example, doing some household task, but not want this discussed openly in order that the parent not feel he or she is being treated as no longer capable. Similarly, on other occasions, actions may be performed without discussion in order to ensure that conflict does not arise as a consequence. As Finch and Mason write, 'formulating clear intentions should be considered part of the process of negotiating family obligations, though implicit rather than explicit' (ibid. 74).

Finch and Mason's final category — 'non-decisions' — refers to negotiations which arise without open discussion or people forming clear intentions. Here, in the absence of overt agreement or a consciously developed strategy, what occurs is one party being recognized by all as the 'obvious' person to provide whatever help is necessary for the relative. For all intents and purposes, it appears that the arrangement just emerges. Yet typically, behind this emergence lies a whole range of biographical and contextual considerations. In particular, gender is important, with Finch and Mason suggesting that routinely it is women who end up providing support when the negotiations are of a non-decision sort (ibid. 77). Because of their relationship history, their caring skills, and the configuration of their other responsibilities, women are often defined as self-evidently the most appropriate person to provide support, especially with regard to the personal care of elderly parents. In particular, because of their greater involvement over the life-course with domestic and relational matters, the premiss that slowly emerges, without need for discussion, is that a particular female will be available and willing to provide the necessary care when it is needed.

There are three points to make about 'non-decisions'. First, it is likely that a good number of these types of decisions remain unacknowledged because of their very obviousness. As Finch and Mason write: 'implicit processes tend to be more difficult to identify and recount than more concrete examples of open discussion' (ibid. 75). Second, 'non-decisions' are often an (unrecognized) element of more overt negotiations which effectively frame the boundaries of the decisions that are being made. In other words, who accepts what sort of responsibility for providing support for elderly parents (or other relatives) is usually not a matter debated from a blank starting-point. The nature of the existing relationships and responsibilities people have will play a part in how the provision of future support is debated and organized. And thirdly, those who accrue responsibility for providing elderly parents and others with support may feel constrained and 'put upon' through their special commitment being unrecognized by others who could take responsibility, but nonetheless they tend to share the logic of the non-decision and be willing to provide the support required. Otherwise, the non-decision is likely to be contested at some level, and so become an issue to be more openly debated rather than remaining as a matter of 'non-decision'.

However the negotiations are patterned, not all eligible kin end up providing the same degree of support or care. Some may simply refuse to countenance any significant involvement. More usually, though, in the process of the negotiations some people are able to proffer reasons why they cannot be expected to help as much as others. They are, in Finch and Mason's terms, able to come up with 'legitimate excuses' that other kin accept, albeit at times grudgingly and with some residual resentment. There are a range of such excuses which are considered legitimate, though the legitimacy they are accorded varies depending on the specific circumstances of the issue in question, the history of relationships built up over time, and the situations of those other kin involved in the negotiations.

The 'excuses' which Finch and Mason found were given legitimacy in their study were quite varied. They detail five different forms. First, there were issues to do with *employment*. By and large, and with an element of gender difference, people are not expected to give up their jobs in order to provide support for elderly parents (or other kin), especially if the household's welfare depends primarily on the income earned. Second, people who had other *family commitments* were often able to get these accepted as reasons why they should be less rather than more involved in care provision. Thus the educational careers of adolescent children might be given priority over caring for an elderly parent; or already providing care for, say, a disabled child would be considered a legitimate reason for not taking on responsibility for the welfare of elderly parents. Third, there is the issue of *competence*. Some people, especially males, are not seen as having the necessary skills or personality to provide care adequately. Fourth, *geographical distance* acts as a block on the degree of support people can offer. Other things being equal, people are not generally expected to disrupt their lives by moving in order to become more involved in care-giving. And finally, a *lack of resources* can also be accepted as a legitimate reason for not providing support. For example, lack of money, lack of time, or lack of transport can be reasons why some people cannot get involved in caring for infirm parents as heavily as they otherwise might be expected to (ibid. 102–12).

The point here is not that people simply state these excuses and consequently escape responsibility for providing support for elderly parents when they need it. The issue is much more that in the implicit or explicit negotiations which occur about who should provide what sort of support, these types of factor are typically built into the decisions which are made. As noted, these decisions often get made over a period of time. Over this time, the types of issue discussed here are brought into the negotiations, accepted as legitimate at some level, and thus frame whatever it is that, in each case, is seen as the most appropriate and reasonable solution. Moreover, while such factors as these are generally given credence as legitimate excuses, this does not mean they are drawn on equally by all. Some people do become involved in care for elderly parents even though one or more of the circumstances discussed above apply. Finch and Mason's research, like that of others, details a good number of instances where individuals take on more of the care burden than they could 'reasonably' be expected to (Briggs and Oliver, 1985; Ungerson, 1987).

It is important to recognize the significance of time in the negotiations that occur. No decision is made separately from ones that have gone before. Indeed, what seems to occur is a process by which some people become committed to providing support. Decisions or commitments made at time 1 cannot easily be reneged on, and usually there is no desire to do so unless other circumstances have changed significantly. But commitments made at time 1 have consequences for the decisions reached at times 2, 3, and 4. That is, as people accept responsibilities for providing support, so each earlier acceptance becomes part of the context in which later negotiations occur.

And in turn the provision of support has repercussions for the ways in which those providing it define themselves and for the ways in which

others see them. Such commitments, in other words, are not just prom-
ises or intentions about caring behaviour; they also carry a moral value.
They become one of the elements which make up the individual's
identity, and provide her or him with a sense of their moral worth. Finch
and Mason (1993) argue that these identities are built up over the life-
course. Within the kin group, and outside it, people's identity and sense
of self evolve through the types of relationship they develop and the
decisions they make about the kin exchanges and support they are
willing to participate in. Gradually their identity takes its shape, not
irreversibly, but with sufficient force to constrain future actions if they
do not wish to lose face in later exchanges. It is because these processes
of identity formation within the kin network occur over time that Finch
and Mason (1993) can talk of responsibilities being generated through
negotiation, even when there is no direct discussion about a particular
decision at the time it is made. The negotiations can be implicit because
they are framed by the commitments people are recognized to have
made at earlier times.

Material considerations

This chapter has been concerned with the ways in which responsibilities to provide support for elderly parents in particular can best be
understood. There is one major change occurring in British society
which has implications for elderly people's care and has so far not been
discussed. This concerns the changing pattern of wealth-holding which
has developed in the second half of the twentieth century, particularly
as a result of the growth of owner-occupation. In 1945, approximately a
quarter of all households were in the owner-occupied sector. Fifty years
later two-thirds are. What this has meant is that for the first time in
history, large portions of the population have significant amounts of
property to bequeath on their deaths. Typically this property is inherited by their children, who are likely themselves to be established in
middle age at the time. This raises the question of the relationship
between property, inheritance, and care provision.

In some cases, of course, the capital accrued from owner-occupation
may be used directly to pay for care provision, either in a residential
home or in a nursing home. The costs of the latter especially can eat
quite quickly into the wealth accumulated through owner-occupation
and other forms of saving over a lifetime. But where it does not, the
interesting kinship question is whether people are rewarded through

inheritance for the informal support they have provided in their parents' old age. How do material considerations enter into the types of negotiation discussed above? Or does the principle of broadly equal inheritance for all children remain even when there has been differential care and support provided? And how often are negotiations framed around issues of inheritance, either implicitly or explicitly?

Currently these issues are ones we know rather little about, though some research attention is now being directed at them. However, if we remember the work of Bell (1968) and Leonard (1980) discussed in Chapters 3 and 5, it would seem likely that material issues play some part in the exchanges which occur when older people with resources need increasing amounts of care. However, the idea that all children should be treated 'fairly' and receive broadly equal shares of their parents' estates also seems to be a moral principle to which people are strongly attached. Of course, one of the issues here is what being treated 'fairly' actually means in different contexts. It might well be that over time, different norms emerge over fair treatment as the numbers of people with significant levels of capital to bequeath through owner-occupation increases.

Thus, for example, it might be that some older people hold open discussions — negotiations — with their children about the distribution of inheritance money based on the provision of support in later years. This, though, seems unlikely in most cases, given that death and inheritance appear to be spoken about rather little between the generations. However, there are other ways in which individuals may receive material benefits from being the primary carer. First, of course, there are gifts and payments made while the elderly parent is alive. Agreements may be struck, again implicitly or explicitly, over the gifts, payments, and exchanges that are appropriate if care is being given. Second, in some instances the main carer will become the main beneficiary because she or he has lived in the parental home throughout their lives. Other resources may be divided between other children, but the house will be given to the child living there to ensure their security. Thirdly, when a parent moves to live with a child, some of the money realized through the sale of the parental home may be used to purchase a larger house or to build a 'granny flat' attached to it. On the parent's death, the property continues to belong to the child in question rather than its increased value being divided between the sibling set.

As stated, though, at present rather little is known about how these situations are handled in different families and kin groups. Research is certainly needed on how different packages of care provision — informally provided v. market provided; household care v. residential care;

individual responsibility v. shared responsibilities; etc. — affect the expression of kinship solidarity. What types of negotiation occur? Who is involved in them? How explicit are they? How do older people use the threat or promise of inheritance to protect their interests? Do negotiations about caring responsibilities differ at all when there are significant levels of inheritance involved as against instances where there is no property to bequeath? To what extent are decisions to move to residential or nursing homes influenced by calculations about inheritance? These and other questions like them are important not just for understanding kinship behaviour but also because they affect social policy. Equally though, social policies — especially those relating to questions of the conditions under which the State will pay for care — are likely to influence the decisions individuals and families reach.

Conclusion

This chapter has been concerned with the ways in which responsibilities between kin are enacted, paying special heed to the circumstances of older people who through infirmity need increased levels of care and support. Here there is a transformation of what until this stage of the life-course has been the normal pattern of exchange between the generations. Independence — so important in the construction of adulthood — is undermined as the support given becomes more unilateral. Drawing on the work of Qureshi and Walker (1989), I argued that close kin, especially children, are normally seen as having some responsibility for providing support for their parents when they become infirm, especially if there is no spouse to provide care. This is taken to represent the expression at this life stage of the 'diffuse enduring solidarity' discussed in the previous chapter. Qureshi and Walker (1989) were able to produce a hierarchical schema that indicated where responsibility is seen as normally falling which appears to reflect a broad consensus.

Where there is less clarity or consensus is over exactly what the responsibilities of different kin are. Following the perspective developed by Finch and Mason (Finch, 1989; Finch and Mason, 1993) — undoubtedly the most important examination of British kinship to be produced in recent years — it was argued that kinship action cannot be understood as simply the application of well-specified 'rules'. The processes are more subtle than this. In particular, what appears to occur within kin networks, but especially between primary kin, is a process of negotiation, often tacit but on occasion becoming overt. Such negotiation builds on individuals' previous kinship actions and commitments, the other responsibilities and obligations they have, and the resource constraints they face. Through these processes, the responsibilities of different members of the kin network get assigned, sometimes accompanied by a degree of resentment, in ways which usually embody the sense of obligation there is between kin but which cannot be properly understood as simply norm-governed or rule-based. Kinship obligations and responsibilities are actively worked out, not passively enacted.

Further reading

Janet Finch and Jennifer Mason's study, *Negotiating Family Responsibilities* (1993), examines the nature of kinship obligation and responsibility in contemporary Britain. Based on an imaginative research design, it provides a great deal of information on the ways in which people understand their kinship ties.

There are numerous studies of the kinship support older people receive when they become infirm. Hazel Qureshi and Alan Walker's *The Caring Relationship: Elderly People and their Families* (1989) is particularly good. Jane Lewis and Barbara Meredith's *Daughters Who Care: Daughters Caring for Mothers at Home* (1988) is also very informative. While not solely concerned with the elderly population, Fred St Leger and Norman Gillespie's *Informal Welfare in Belfast: Caring Communities?* (1991) is useful for providing a detailed account of the role of kin and other informal relationships in giving support.

Chapter Seven

Friendship: Class, Gender, and Status

The purpose of this chapter and the next is to consider ties of friendship, both for their own sake and to highlight similarities and differences in friendship and kinship relations. Those who study kinship often comment on the paucity of contemporary studies. However, in comparison to friendship we know a great deal about kinship ties, especially with regard to Britain. There are very few studies in sociology (or other social-science disciplines) which are explicitly concerned with friendship. In the main, what knowledge we have has to be garnered from studies in which friendship is an element of the research concerns, but rarely a dominant one. There are also studies from other countries, particularly the United States, though how easily these can be 'translated' to a British context remains a moot point. Cultural and social-structural variables influence the ways friendships are patterned, so what is true in one country may not be the case in another.

In previous chapters examining kinship, it has been possible to give some information about the number of kin individuals on average have and to indicate which categories of kin are personally and socially the most significant. This is because kinship ties are defined principally by genealogical connection — blood and marriage — rather than by the quality or character of the personal relationships involved. Knowing about a kinship connection of itself tells you nothing about its social content. With friendship the situation is quite different. Friends are only defined on the basis of the relationships which exist. While there may occasionally be conflict between friends, the categorization of someone as a friend is based on the quality of the bond that there is. There is no other criterion. Neighbours live near you, workmates work with you, kin are part of your wider family — in each of these cases you may or may not have active relationships with those involved, you may or may not like them. With friendship, this is not the case. The criteria for membership of the category depend very much on the relationship which has developed between you.

This may seem obvious and hardly worth mentioning. However, it does have important consequences for the analysis of the ties. In particular, the categorization of others as 'friends' becomes much more complicated, and as a consequence so too does the comparison of different people's friendship patterns. At the heart of the complexity is the lack of firmly agreed and socially acknowledged criteria for what makes a person a friend. Indeed, the criteria used are themselves contextual. That is, whereas someone may be referred to as a friend in one setting, the label may seem less appropriate in a different context. The boundaries drawn around the category are not rigid; there are no clear-cut lines around who should be included and who excluded. Some people are clearly friends; others are 'sort-of' friends but not quite fully so (Allan, 1979; Adams, 1989). To see this, try the following exercise.

Activity 7.1 Identifying Friends

Make a list of all the people you know in one or two different settings, such as college or school, work, or some club you belong to. Now go through these lists and see which people on it you would define as a friend.

Now try to write down the criteria you used in making the decisions. Think in particular of those relationships you had difficulty in deciding about — those people who you know who are 'sort-of' or 'well, maybe they are but...' friends. Why did you have a problem in deciding whether they were friends or not? What were the conflicting issues that concerned you?

When you have done this for yourself, approach someone else you know and ask them about their friendships. Again, listen here to any difficulties they have in categorizing their different social contacts and see if you can make explicit the criteria they are implicitly using to decide.

The point of this exercise has been to illustrate the problems that arise simply in counting the number of friends a person has and making comparisons between people. But the situation is actually still more complicated than this suggests.

As well as difficulties in deciding who qualifies as a friend on an individual-relationship level, there are also differences in the ways that different groups within British culture organize their friendlike ties. These differences make the label given these relationships problematic, especially when researchers attempt to gather the 'facts' of friendship. In particular, various community, occupational, and family studies have indicated that there are class differences in the ways in which sociability is organized. (See Allan, 1979, for a review of some of these.) These differences lead to the middle class claiming more friends in general, with this sometimes being taken to suggest that the working class are less socially active, or rather that their informal activities are dominated by kinship. These issues are of some consequence for understanding patterns of friendship, and indeed, by implication, patterns of kinship. They are thus worth discussing more fully.

Class differences in friendship

We will start by considering the ways in which the middle class typically develop their friendships. In order to do this it is necessary to distinguish between the relationships people have and the contexts in which interactions occur. Relationships refer to the continuing bonds that exist between people, each of which comes with a distinct history and an implicit frame of reference. That is, we carry with us notions of what each of our relationships is like; what types of expectations we have about them; what obligations, responsibilities, and demands are legitimate and relevant to them. These are not immutable; they change as the relationship develops and as our social circumstances alter. Nonetheless, at any given time, in order to manage or 'do' the relationship, we have a broad idea, a shared understanding, of what it is that is relevant to that relationship and how it is ordered. In this sense we can think in terms of the boundaries which are constructed around relationships. While not absolutely fixed or rigid, these boundaries of relevance provide for an understanding of how the relationship is defined, of the framing which is placed around it.

Part of this framing concerns the contexts in which interactions occur. Obviously in order to develop a friendship, or any other informal relationship, there has to be some context in which you initially meet one another. Occasionally this may not involve face-to-face interaction, as for example with pen-pals or e-mail relationships. However, in the great majority of cases, initial contact is direct; the relationship is initiated through your both being in the same setting at the same time. What matters is how the relationship develops after this. The contextual basis of the relationship may remain static. That is, you continue to see one another within this context without making any effort to activate the relationship in other settings. Alternatively you may choose to extend the implicit boundaries of the relationship by fostering interaction elsewhere. Someone met at work may be invited home or you may arrange to go for a meal or to a sports event with them. The wider the contexts of interaction, the less the relationship is likely to be defined in terms of its initial context, and indeed the more likely the language of 'friendship' will be considered relevant to it. What starts off as a colleague tie gets gradually transformed into a friendship one. Importantly, the boundaries constructed around a relationship do not only refer to the contexts of interaction seen as relevant. They can also be conceptualized as referring to the types of exchange which are defined as relevant to the relationship, for example, emotional support; shared activities; sociability; the sharing of confidences. However, here the discussion will be restricted to the contexts in which relationships are developed.

The middle-class pattern of friendship formation is quite clear and essentially the dominant one in terms of what friendship is taken to mean. Essentially when people are met who are liked, the common pattern is for the relationship to be developed by extending its boundaries through involving the other person in other social contexts. As above, a colleague who is liked on a work basis is asked for a drink, invited home, or accompanied to some entertainment. As the person comes to be known better through interaction in such different settings, so the relationship is transformed into a friendship. The use of the home for entertaining is particularly significant in this pattern, as involving the relationship in the home — the individual's private arena — symbolizes the independence of the relationship from the initial context which defined it. It clearly gives priority to the relationship over its context, especially when the home becomes routinized as a setting for interaction.

In contrast, working-class sociability has traditionally not been routinely organized in this same way. From the various evidence available, and it must be recognized that much of it is now quite dated, it appears that less emphasis is placed on extending the contextual boundaries of relationships in line with the dominant middle-class pattern. Instead the tendency has been more for non-kin relationships to remain bounded by the initial setting of interaction even when particular individuals are significant people in one another's personal networks. Thus, by and large, workmates are not seen elsewhere unless they also happen to share other activities in common; people from a leisure or sporting club are not routinely invited home; neighbours are only rarely included in other sociable activities.

Thus generally there tends to be a greater emphasis placed on specific contexts, with relationships, in the language used above, being more bounded. They are not developed by encouraging interaction in a wider range of settings. However, it needs to be recognized, in line with the arguments of Chapter 2, that patterns of sociability are not static. They get modified in line with wider social and economic shifts. Thus there is some evidence that the home is being used more frequently in working-class sociability than in the past, in line with changing definitions of marriage and domestic space (Franklin, 1989; Binns and Mars, 1984). Nonetheless, many working-class sociable ties still appear to be more tightly framed than their middle-class equivalents.

Where relationships are more contextually bound, they are not always defined as 'friendships'. The issue here is not that these relationships are of little significance. In any social setting some ties will be more important to the individual than others; some people will be liked more than others, found to be more compatible and trusted more. But the tendency is for even these relationships to remain more tightly bounded than equivalent middle-class relationships. As a result, there is more hesitancy about using the label 'friendship' to describe these ties. Because they are more contextually bounded, they fit less easily into cultural ideas of what friendship means. Instead, other labels are often used to describe them, with 'mate' being a particularly common one.

The term 'mate' is often used in friendship talk but it is not altogether synonymous with 'friend'. In particular, it is used to convey personal solidarity and commitment but of a different form to 'friend'. The key difference is the one referred to in the above discussion. Whereas 'friend' celebrates a specific relationship over and above any specific contexts, the idea of 'mate' is often linked more fully with a given context. Certainly, this is an important aspect in much working-class use of the term. Mates are, in other words, people who are seen in particular places, be these pubs, work, social clubs, or whatever, with interaction predominantly being restricted to that setting. What this means is that within the symbolic construction of these ties location defines the relationship, rather than the relationship being seen as its own end. The relationships are important but they arise from common participation in a social arena (or context) rather than being developed in a more independent, 'free-floating' fashion.

One consequence of this is that these relationships appear to be less purposeful, less planned than typical middle-class friendships. They arise through participation in the context rather than through deliberate arrangement. People are seen routinely; they will be there tomorrow, next week, or whenever, just as they have been in the past. However, the explicit focus remains framed by the activity rather than the relationship. Within this framing the individual relationship comes less to the forefront; what matters is the shared participation in a given activity, not the commitment to a relationship for its own sake. This is a subtle distinction in practice, but nonetheless symbolically an important one. Equally, because of the emphasis in the construction of these ties on context, the relationships are often viewed as more collective than middle-class friendships are. While interaction between such friends often occurs with others, the primacy given to context in mateships means that these ties are rarely seen as exclusive. Rather, they tend to be conceived as more open, often occurring in group contexts even though within that group some ties are recognized by all as being stronger than others. Indeed, while the term 'mate' is a common enough one, it is frequently used in the plural.

Status and the balance of friendship

Now, the obvious questions are why these differences arise and what their consequences are for studying friendship. In quite large part, the answers lie in the common character of virtually all 'friend-type' relationships. Friendship, in whatever form it takes, is defined as a relationship between equals. That is, within friendship there is little sense of social hierarchy or status difference. Instead the emphasis is placed firmly on similarity and equivalence. Whatever the social differences outside the tie, at the core of friendship is the notion that friends regard and treat one another as equals within it. Friendships in which there are marked inequalities or in which one side continually lays claim to social superiority over the other will not last long. But there is another, arguably more important sense in which friendships are ties of equality. This concerns the balance of exchange which arises in these relationships. Essentially, friends are not supposed to take more from one another than they give. If one friend does a favour for the other, the implicit assumption is that the other will be willing to do something equivalent in the future. Over time, the exchanges which occur should even out. This does not mean that the exchanges are always balanced or that immediate ways are found for repaying favours. What it means is that exchanges are reciprocated so that overall neither side is seen as taking advantage of the other or of using their friendship solely for their own gain. While circumstance can lead to exceptions, for most ties to be seen as ones of friendship there must be a semblance of middle- or longer-term balance of exchange in them. Where this is not the case the friendships are likely to break down.

Thus friends (or mates or whatever) need to ensure that reciprocity is maintained within these ties if they are not to be seen as breaking the implicit rules governing them. In order to maintain their reputation and self-esteem, they will not wish to become inappropriately indebted to their friends. Yet maintaining reciprocity is not always a straightforward matter. In particular, for those with fewest resources, a key issue in managing sociability may be to ensure that the demands made on resources by the requirement for reciprocity are not too great. This is not an issue with kinship to anything like the same degree, as these relationships are not based upon equality or the same level of reciprocity. But with friendships, the need for reciprocity is an important principle. The management and control of reciprocity, and consequently of the demands which can be made of you, thus comes to play a key role in the organization of sociability with non-kin.

Here we can see why the class-based differences in sociability discussed above arise. Whereas in general the middle class have sufficient resources so as not to need to worry unduly about reciprocation within friendship, within working-class culture there is a greater need to limit the possible claims that might be made on scarce resources. Emphasizing context over individual relationships and not extending the boundaries of non-kin ties is one way of managing this. Essentially, where interaction is defined as being as much about the setting in which it occurs as about the relationships it involves, then provided individuals have control over their entrances and exits to those settings they will also have greater control over the call made upon their resources. Moreover, as Oxley (1974) has demonstrated in his study of inequality in a small Australian mining town, the emphasis on context renders it easier to make issues outside of that context of little importance. Hence status or other differentials are played down. What matters are the activities of the setting rather than the social characteristics of those involved. Where the relationship is weighted above the context, as in middle-class friendships, it is far harder to ignore differentials of wealth, status, power, or income.

Because of these differences in the ways in which non-kin ties are constructed, it is not easy to compare data on friendship. Often empirical research concentrates on people's 'closest' or 'best' friends, asking them to name, say, the four or six friends they see most frequently or feel they can confide in most. Equally, when people are questioned about their friendships, they often assume a rather 'tighter' notion of friendship than when friendship is not the specific topic of discussion.

Thus, people who may be referred to in passing as a friend in other situations may not be categorized as such in a research setting. This applies especially when the label 'friend' seems somewhat inapplicable anyway, as is the case with those relationships which seem to fit the category 'mate' better. Thus some of the differences which are found in the number of friends different people have may stem from the different ways they typically organize their non-kin ties. A brother is a brother, and we all generally mean the same by this. A friend, though, is not always just a friend!

Activity 7.2 The Concept of Friendship

If, as suggested in Activity 7.1, you asked others about their friendship patterns, how did they categorize different relationships? Did they, as suggested here, draw on a relatively 'tight' idea of friendship? To what extent did you feel that making 'friendship' the topic affected what they understood by the term?

The issue of equality in friendship is not just a matter of reciprocity and balance of exchange. Another factor which has been touched on above but which is worth fuller consideration here concerns who friends are. A good deal of research in this country and elsewhere has shown that typically friends occupy similar social positions to one another. They tend, for example, to be of the same age, have similar class positions, to be the same gender, and to occupy similar positions in the life-course. This is not absolute, of course. There are plenty of counter-examples. Yet the tendency is marked. As with similarity between marriage partners, this is not surprising. After all, if people are to become friends they need to meet in settings broadly amenable to the development of friendship and, by and large, social organization ensures that we tend mainly to meet people like us under such conditions. That is, friendships tend to mirror the status divisions which arise in the society more generally.

This status 'homophily', as it is known in the research literature, is itself closely related to the issues of reciprocity and equivalence of exchange mentioned earlier. When people are in a broadly similar social and economic position to one another and where they share a similar life-style, not only are they likely to have more interests and commitments in common, but equally they are likely to have broadly similar resources. Thus, maintaining approximately equal forms of exchange creates relatively few difficulties. If there are wide disparities in the resources each friend has, then maintaining a level of symmetry in the exchanges becomes far more problematic. Indeed, where such differences arise, it may not even be clear what counts as equivalence. Under these circumstances, it is likely that the friendship tie will gradually become less active unless both sides make a special effort to sustain it despite the differences there are. As mentioned earlier, there are contexts in which this can be achieved, like the one studied by Oxley (1974) mentioned earlier, but more generally friendships marked by social difference will fade.

Gender and friendship

Just as issues of class and status impinge on patterns of friendship, so does gender (O'Connor, 1992). Indeed, Robert Bell (1981) suggested that gender is probably the most significant of all social divisions in shaping friendship. Traditionally the argument has been that men are more active sociably and have more friends than women. Some sociobiologists have even gone so far as to suggest that men have a greater biological propensity for friendship as a consequence of their role within hunting and gathering societies (e.g. Tiger, 1969). While such arguments need not detain us here, it is important to recognize that in many respects men and women occupy quite distinct social and economic positions and thus have different opportunities to develop and activate their friendships. This does not of course mean that all women or all men have equivalent friendship patterns, distinct from those of the other gender. Gender is only one factor influencing friendship patterns, a point which will be developed in Chapter 8. But it is of major consequence in structuring the experiences people have and consequently the space there is in their lives for friendships.

Gender differences in friendship patterns appear at quite a young age and seem to be tied in with children's developing sense of gender identity. Studies in Britain and America have suggested that from quite a young age boys have larger friendship networks than girls. However, girls appear to be more intimate with their friends, being more willing to confide and discuss their fears and anxieties (Dickens and Perlman, 1981). This of course is in line with the differential encouragement boys and girls receive from parents and other adults in their lives to express emotion. It also reflects the greater emphasis in boys' play on shared activities and 'doing' in contrast to girls' greater concentration on what can be termed 'relational' matters. Such differences appear to mirror later life to the extent that men's lives are more 'public' than women's, bringing them into contact with a wide range of others through their work and leisure. Many women in contrast have less extensive social participation, but undertake work inside and outside the home in which the management of relationships is central.

The issue here is that people's patterns of friendship are likely to be related to the wider experiences they have (Hess, 1979; Allan, 1989; O'Connor, 1992). Men frequently have more time and financial resources to devote to sociability than women, because of their role within the domestic and paid division of labour. They also have readier access to a range of clubs and organizations, including for example pubs and sports, geared to sociable activities of different forms. But if men do typically have more opportunity for social participation, it does not follow that they therefore have more friends, especially close friends. The argument developed by a number of writers is that men's position within the social and economic structure allows sociable relations to be formed, but at the same time restricts the level of intimacy and disclosure of self these relationships involve (Pleck, 1976; Hess, 1979; Allan, 1989; Reid and Fine, 1992).

Thus men are frequently involved in sociable activities with others which are geared around quite specific activities and pastimes. However, many, though not all, of these relationships are likely to be quite shallow in terms of the degree to which significant personal issues and concerns are discussed. This is highly consonant with dominant ideologies of masculinity. However much cultural images of masculinity are altering, the dominant forms still give little emphasis to the expression of more tender and compassionate feelings outside romantic relationships, instead giving greater legitimacy to 'harder' emotions like aggression and anger. This is reflected in the construction of men's friendships, with these relationships not being founded on a strong expectation that men will confide in one another or discuss personal problems. Paul Wright (1982) expresses this well when he writes of men's friendships being 'side by side'. What he is highlighting here, especially for 'ordinary' rather than 'close' friendships, is the way in which the prioritizing of activities and 'doing' structures the boundaries of the ties so that more intimate matters are effectively ruled out of court.

In contrast, Wright characterizes women's friendships as more 'face to face', with intimacy frequently playing a larger part within them. Because of the character of their domestic and paid labour, many women have less opportunity to develop sociable ties than men. This does not necessarily mean they have fewer friendships, though, for as suggested earlier, not all sociable contacts are transformed into recognized friendships. (The research evidence on the number of friends men and women claim — most of which is American — suggests the differences are relatively minor, but that other factors like class, age, and family course position influence this. See, for example, Fischer and Oliker, 1983.) On the other hand, these same factors which constrain women's social participation also tend to infuse the character of their friendships with a different dynamic to men's.

Just as men's social location influences their friendship behaviour, so women's location affects the way they are with their friends. In particular, their responsibility for the management of relationships within the home (and elsewhere) results in the discussion of relationship issues being given a higher priority in their friendships (Oliker, 1989). While men may disparage much women's relational talk as gossip, it can more accurately be seen as a reflection of the concerns which arise through their role in the division of labour. Confiding in one another about their different personal relationships, seeking advice, and discussing problems is, in other words, as consonant with their personal and social identity as it is discrepant with men's. Here of course it is important that the dominant construction of femininity does encourage closeness, empathy, and the expression of feelings (O'Connor, 1992).

There is a danger of overemphasizing gender differences in friendship content. Not all men's friendships are lacking in intimacy, nor do women spend all their time talking about such matters (Nardi, 1992). Moreover, it is evident that many other factors affect the way in which friendships are organized aside from gender. Some of these will be discussed in the next chapter, where the issue of friendship and identity will also be considered more fully. However, the research evidence available, much of it American, does support the idea that men's and women's friendships are typically constructed somewhat differently. The key issue, though, is the more general one: that friendship is not independent of other aspects of people's social and economic lives. Rather, the patterns of people's friendships reflect and are built around their social locations and social identities.

Friendship and change

It is important to recognize that friendship networks are quite different from kinship networks in the degree of change which occurs within them. Whereas kinship ties, and especially primary kinship ties, generally continue in some form or other, change in friendship is routine and normal. Certainly some friendships are long-term, a few even lasting a lifetime. The majority, though, are not like this. Instead they wax and wane. They are active for some period in our lives but then gradually become less significant. While occasionally they may end as a result of some conflict or disagreement, more usually they slowly fade as people's circumstances alter. The people involved see one another less, and over time fewer attempts are made to keep in touch. Eventually even Christmas cards, the most evident symbol of friendship for many people, may no longer be exchanged. New friends replace these now moribund ones in our lives. This process is entirely routine. It is not an indication that these friendships were somehow flawed; it is the consequence of the way the ties are socially organized.

With 'mateships', as distinct from friendships, the process is even more marked. Because in the ways discussed above, mateships are tied to specific social contexts, these ties usually end whenever one or other of the mates are no longer involved in the activities of that context. If people change job, if they move house, if they no longer go to the same club or pub, then the rationale for the relationships they were involved in there disappears. At times some effort may be made to keep in touch; on occasions visits back will be made or other meetings arranged (Williams, 1983), but by and large the ties cease once the context which defined them is no longer an active part of people's routines. Again, the recognition of this — of the power of context over individuality within the construction of the relationship — makes the use of the description 'friend' seem less appropriate than that of 'mate'.

But under what circumstances do friendships fade? As with mateships, the simple answer is that friendships end when people's circumstances change so that maintaining the relationship becomes more difficult. If, for example, people move to another area or if their work begins to make much heavier demands on their time, then it is likely that a number of their friendships will become less active. However, it seems that a major reason why friendships end is not just for this type of reason, but more interestingly because a change in people's social position often makes the equality which lies at the heart of friendship difficult to manage (Adams, 1987). Whereas once there was a relatively easy balance within the relationship, this can be altered by status changes so that the management of the tie becomes more complex.

The sorts of changes in social position which can affect friendships are various. One important one concerns people's position in the life-course. Typically there appears to be a change in friendship patterns when people get married, for example. Their previous friendships with other single people often seem to become less central in their lives, tending to be replaced by other couple friendships (Cohen, 1992). This is not altogether surprising. Often couples are attempting to construct a marital relationship in which 'togetherness' and mutual involvement is paramount. A part of this is sharing leisure and sociability, so that having friends in common, rather than their own separate sets, is of consequence. If their friends are still single, managing these ties can become difficult. The marriage begins to alter the solidarity that previously existed between the friends, the activities they shared may no longer be so appropriate, and finding a way of balancing the demands that are made can create tension. Similar shifts occur in friendships when children are born. Old activities become more problematic. Especially in their early years, children set a different agenda and a different time-scale for sociable activities. They tend to dominate the activities of the parents in ways that make developing and servicing friendships with others who also have children simpler. Gradually, older friends in different life-course phases become less involved and are replaced by others who share a similar social location.

Some of the most interesting research on the impact of life-course changes on friendships comes from studies of those whose marriages have ended, either through divorce or with widowhood. What these studies reveal is the lack of ease which people feel in their previous friendships. While in the short term these existing friendships can be very supportive, in the longer run the lack of symmetry in the familial positions occupied makes their continuation somewhat problematic. There is usually nothing sudden in this, more a gradual shift, a gradual change in the level of involvement. Thus now-single people report finding the management of reciprocity in these relationships difficult. Where interaction was couple-based, the rhythm of the relationship is thrown out of balance. The implicit 'rules' which governed interaction are harder to apply. Thus conversation is less balanced; reciprocity is harder to achieve, for example in simple matters like buying rounds of drinks; there is a sense of being treated as the odd one out; and so forth. At times those involved report feeling unintentionally stigmatized because of the concern their still-married friends are showing them (Hart, 1976; Milardo, 1987). By themselves none of these things are important, but collectively they have an impact and result in the relationships becoming that much more difficult to sustain. The consequence is that people's friendship networks gradually alter. Often they may become smaller, especially where there are few others in a structurally similar position, e.g. widowers in later life (Blau, 1961; Bankoff, 1981). But mainly they tend to become dominated more by people who share the experiences that the individual has of no longer being married. This is not invariable, and certainly does not lead to a complete change in friendships; all it means is that a gradual shift occurs, a gradual transformation in who the individual comes to rely on most.

Equally, though, friendships alter when other aspects of an individual's social location change. For example, when people gain promotion at work it can have an impact on their friendship ties, especially, though not only, with any of their colleagues they regard as friends or mates. Here similar processes are at work. When one person is in a different position within a hierarchy, if they have a degree of authority over the others, if their earning capacity and life-style are altered, then maintaining the friendships in their previous forms is no longer as straightforward as it was. In these circumstances it is still possible to sustain the balance in the relationship, and all sides may agree that the change in question is not going to affect their friendship. This after all is what the ideological construction of friendship would require: friendship is not about status hierarchy or difference; it is about solidarity on the basis of liking and trust. Changes in one side's position should not affect these matters. However, in practice, ideology notwithstanding, they usually do. As with change in family circumstance, the relationships slowly become less active; gradually new friends who are more compatible with the new status and developed life-style take their place. The process can be more marked, but also less problematic, if the change has involved geographical mobility. Here distance makes the idea that the friendships have not been affected by the change of lesser consequence, as the change is so evidently 'external' to the tie.

Conclusion

This chapter has been concerned with the concept of friendship and with the ways in which sociable ties are routinely organized. As well as pointing out some of the class and gender differences which exist in friendship patterns, it has focused on the role of equality and reciprocity within these ties. There is no doubt that maintaining friendships in the face of significant inequalities, whether these be of wealth, status, interest, or family position, is actually quite difficult. These ties normally depend on a taken-for-granted, unproblematic reciprocity and equivalence which is far easier to manage when there are no 'external' differences to get in its way. Because of this, changes in friendship networks are common. As people's position within the social structure alters, so gradually do their friendships. This is a normal process, and not one which indicates any inadequacy within those ties.

The next chapter develops some of the points made in this one. In particular, it is concerned with the ways in which friendship links up with broader aspects of social structure. In doing this, it examines the 'space' there is in people's lives for friendship; how, in other words, other aspects of their social and economic circumstances impinge on their opportunities for sociable involvement. It also discusses what role friendship plays within social life. Are these ties just ones of sociability, or do they have other consequences for the ways in which we manage our various activities? In a nutshell, are they socially redundant or socially useful?

Further reading

Friendships Between Women (1992) by Pat O'Connor provides a very good summary of many of the issues considered in this chapter (and the next), focusing, as the title indicates, on women's friendships. Peter Willmott's *Friendship Networks and Social Support* (1987) also provides a useful review of much of the British research material on the sociology of friendship. In *Good Company: An Anthropological Study of Old People in Groups* (1992), Dorothy Jerrome provides an insightful account of the value of friendship in contemporary society. Many of the points she makes have a far wider relevance than the title indicates.

Chapter Eight

Social Organization and Friendship

Within our culture, friendship is normally seen as a freely chosen, voluntary relationship. Who friends are, what they do together, how the relationship develops is taken to be of concern only to the friends themselves. In the sociological literature, this is often expressed by describing friendship as 'non-institutionalized'. That is, there appear to be no socially agreed rules governing friendship; no strong norms carrying sanctions specifying what is or is not appropriate to the relationship. It is in this sense that friendship is characterized as predominantly a *personal* relationship.

Yet on reflection it is clear that friendship is not *just* a personal tie. There may be no clear-cut rules governing friendship, but there are cultural scripts about the ways in which friend relationships should be structured. For example, as discussed in Chapter 7, friendship is normally taken as a relationship between equals, involving personal compatibility and a broad equivalence of exchange. Moreover, think about what happens when there are rifts between friends. Often each of those involved will discuss what led up to the rift with other friends and implicitly seek their approval for what happened. If there were no agreed principles governing friendship behaviour, such appeals for support or claims that the other person behaved unreasonably would make little sense.

The point here is that friendship — like all informal relationships — is a social as well as a personal relationship. There is certainly more freedom about how friends behave with one another than there is in many more formal relationships which are governed by strongly institutionalized rules, principles, and procedures. Nonetheless friendship is still located within the social realm. Its form is influenced by the wider organization of social life, and it in turn plays a part in maintaining routine social order (Allan and Adams, 1989). The purpose of this chapter is to examine the social dimensions of friendship and to specify the ways in which these ties need to be recognized as more than just personal. In doing this, the chapter will also indicate the broader significance of friendship within social and economic organization.

Friendship in social context

One characteristic of much research into friendship, and in particular that which starts from a psychological framework, is that it tends to isolate particular friendships and analyse their characteristics individually. It thus fails to view friendships from a more structural perspective or to say very much about their social patterning. Yet questions about the ways in which informal relationships are patterned collectively are clearly of importance, as the debate about privatization indicates. A sociological analysis of friendship certainly needs to do more than look at the organization of individual ties. Amongst other issues, it needs to be concerned with the factors which influence an individual's level of social integration, how informal social participation is affected by other responsibilities, activities, and obligations, and what it is that encourages the development of friendships and other equivalent ties.

A central point here is that friendships are not just freely chosen. They are developed and sustained within the wider framework of people's lives. The choices people make, in other words, are constrained by aspects of social organization over which they have relatively little control. One way of perceiving this is to take the notion of 'immediate social environment', a concept first introduced into the sociological literature by Elizabeth Bott in her seminal study *Family and Social Network*, originally published in 1957. While Bott's development of this concept led her to focus on social networks, which in turn proved extremely influential in the formulation of network analysis within social science (see Chapter 9; Wellman, 1988; Scott, 1991), the idea of 'immediate social environment' need not be restricted to a social network approach.

The advantage of the concept of 'immediate social environment' is that it highlights the interplay between the individual, who occupies that environment, and the social structure, which gives that environment its pattern and shape. It provides, in other words, a way of perceiving the individual in a broader context; it offers a mediation between the social and the personal. For these purposes, each individual's immediate social environment can be thought of as comprising the constellation of structural relationships in which she or he is involved. Thus, for example, a person's gender, class location, work situation, domestic and familial position all have an impact on her or his freedom to develop sociable relationships — and other aspects of their apparently personal life — in ways of their own choosing. But they do not do so separately from each other; their impact is collective. It is the overall constellation of these structural features that matters. Together they form the immediate social environment within which each individual makes their choices, apparently freely.

Thus the concept of immediate social environment is useful for allowing us to see that personal relationships are not developed or sustained in a social or economic vacuum. While we certainly make choices about who we want to spend time with, about what we do in our various relationships, and so forth, these choices cannot be understood solely in their own terms. They are made against a wider contextual background — our distinct immediate social environments. For each of us, caught up at any time in our different configurations of commitments, obligations, and responsibilities, our immediate social environments encourage or discourage, facilitate or hinder different patterns of personal relationships from emerging.

This conception of 'immediate social environment' can be linked with the idea of 'personal space' which Rosemary Deem (1982) first used to explore leisure patterns. Deem used the idea of personal space to represent the area in people's lives which they have free for leisure activities. The boundaries around it are all the various demands and restrictions which the individual's position within the social structure generate for her or him. The space that remains once all these other obligations have been met signifies the opportunities which people have available to them for different forms of leisure activities.

Now just as some people have more personal space for leisure than others, so too some people have more space in their lives for developing and servicing friendships. As Hess (1972) has argued, the opportunities an individual has for developing friendships, and the character of those ties, will be shaped by the overall cluster of roles in which that person is incorporated. The argument here is essentially the same. A person's immediate social environment — the personal space they have available — will not only affect the chances people have to meet with others and form sociable ties, it will also colour the content of those ties — the types of activity engaged in, the frequency with which they meet, their degree of involvement, and so forth. While at one level these are clearly matters of individual choice, at the same time those choices are made within the context set by each individual's structural location (Wellman, 1985; Allan, 1989).

Aspects of structural location

It is not possible here to explore fully all the different elements that shape a person's immediate social environment and govern the space they have available for sociability. Instead, this section will concentrate on four aspects of social activity which exert an influence on friendship patterns. These are *work situation*; *gender*; *domestic circumstances*; and *existing friendships*. It must be remembered that these factors do not operate in isolation; it is the interplay of these and other similar elements — their overall constellation — which collectively shapes friendship behaviour. (See Allan, 1989, for a fuller discussion of these issues.)

Work situation

A person's work situation can influence the opportunities they have to meet with others, as well as the resources of time, money, and energy they have for sociability, in a variety of ways. For example, at a basic level, the money available for sociability once other needs have been met is likely to be of some consequence in patterning friendship inter-actions. While common interests shape what friends do together, the nature of those interests is obviously going to be affected by the re-sources they have available. While friends can spend time together without spending much money, many social activities do require some level of expenditure. Even such things as going for a drink or playing sport may, for some, be limited by financial considerations. So too in the last chapter it was suggested that class differences in the organ-ization of sociable ties may well be a consequence of the need to control expenditure.

The demands and organization of a person's work can also pattern sociable relationships, both inside and outside the workplace. For ex-ample, different shift patterns, different levels of physical and mental exertion, and different periods away from home can all have an impact on the extent to which the individual is able and willing to participate sociably with others once they stop work. Along with their domestic commitments, the ways in which their work demands pattern their daily routines will affect the time they have available for sociability and the effort they are prepared to make.

Furthermore, different forms of work provide people with different opportunities for meeting and getting to know others. People working in larger organizations tend to have a wider range of others to develop sociable ties with and also their work usually gives them structured periods for informal interaction. Similarly, some occupations, especially in the professional service sector, require relationships to be built up with a range of customers and clients, some of whom are quite likely to become known personally. But others working in more isolated contexts do not always have equivalent opportunities for developing sociable relationships. The privatized nature of full-time housework, for example, provides far less scope for generating work-based contacts. To a degree, housewives have control over their own timetables, but, with the exception of some aspects of child care, the work itself does not have sociable interaction built into its organization.

Gender

Just as work circumstances can affect opportunities for developing and servicing friendships, so too a person's gender structures the personal space they have for friendship and sociability. Some of the key issues here were discussed in the previous chapter, so there is no need to dwell on them further. It is sufficient to note that the differing roles of men and women within the overall division of paid and unpaid work have major consequences for their social participation. In particular, while the increased participation of married women in employment has opened up possibilities of work-based sociability as well as giving these women some financial independence, for many, combining paid work with continuing domestic responsibilities can leave them with relatively little free time for other non-familial activities. In contrast most men, and single women, have time schedules which allow for more consolidated periods of leisure.

What also matters here, though, is the use to which free time can be put. And generally men have easier access to what can be termed non-domestic arenas of sociability than women. Without so many domestic commitments constraining their time, men are freer to participate in a variety of leisure clubs and associations. Moreover, many of these clubs and societies, while being formally open to both men and women, are actually male-oriented (Hunt and Satterlee, 1986, 1987). Men tend to be more active in them and consequently to have more say over their running. The situation is of course changing, with women participating more than in the past. But even so, it would appear that men have more freedom than women to engage in the more 'sociable' aspects of these activities — for example, to go for a drink after playing some sport or attending a meeting. This difference is compounded by many women's domestic commitments, the differential social norms governing men's and women's drinking patterns, and of course the fear that many women have of being physically assaulted when out alone, especially at night. Thus, for these varied reasons, men generally have greater personal space for developing ties of sociability than women, though of course there is wide variation in this depending on the other factors shaping each individual's immediate social environment.

Domestic circumstances

An individual's domestic circumstances will certainly influence the forms that their friendships take. For example, if they are married, the quality of their marriage will have some impact on the organization of their sociability. If the marriage is one in which the couple typically engage in leisure pursuits together, it is likely most of their friendships will be joint, usually with other couples. If, on the other hand, they have more separate lives, their friendships too are likely to be individually based. Under these circumstances it is less likely that the home will be used for visiting or entertaining. Similarly, other aspects of family life will affect the space available for friendship. The presence of young children will constrain the freedom people have to meet with others sociably, especially if arranging baby-sitting is difficult. Similarly, caring for an elderly relative can have a major impact on the carer's sociable activities and relationships. The fact that responsibility for caring for dependents, whether they be young children or an infirm parent, falls mainly on women rather than men links to the other gender issues discussed above.

As people move through different phases of the life-course, so their personal space for friendship will alter. As suggested, young children have obvious impact on sociability. So too when children mature and become independent, there are increased possibilities for their parents to generate a different pattern of sociability. For women in particular, the lightening of domestic loads makes the management of their different forms of work that much easier. In principle, this has repercussions for the development and servicing of friendships, though importantly, other aspects of their immediate social environment, including the form of their marriage and the history of sociability they have developed, may well constrain the extent to which this happens.

So too, as we saw in the last chapter, if people divorce, their space for friendship is likely to alter quite dramatically, though how this happens will be affected by their gender and any child-care responsibilities they have. Indeed, for men who have previously led relatively independent lives from their spouses, the effects may be minimal, especially if they stay within the same area. They may still be involved in the same work and leisure activities, and so be able to sustain previous sociable patterns. For women with children, the situation may be quite different, with friendship patterns altering significantly as their social, economic, and domestic circumstances change (Milardo, 1987).

Equally, as people age, the opportunities they have for friendship may alter. For some, retirement will allow them more time to spend with friends, without the tiredness or other constraints of work. For many, though, reduced financial circumstances will limit engagement in sociable activities, as will the loss of the social contacts provided through employment. Later, widowhood brings its own consequences, not dissimilar to those of divorce. Infirmity too limits people's opportunities for friendship interaction, as does the number of friends lost through death. Once more, gender can be important here, both because of women's lesser pension rights and because of differential death rates, with men being less likely to be widowed than women (Blieszner and Adams, 1992).

Existing friendships

Finally, consider existing friendships. It is too simple to suggest that friendship circles become 'full' in some direct sense. On the other hand it is clear that there is variation in the extent to which people want to develop new sociable contacts. People in stable social situations, who have, for example, lived in the same area for some period and whose domestic and employment lives are settled, are likely to have built up a network of friends and have relatively little space for new friendships. This does not mean new friendships will not develop, for, as argued in the previous chapter, friendships are dynamic. But it does mean that at any time they are less likely to be looking to develop new ties.

Others, for example those who have recently moved into an area, may be more explicitly wanting to develop new friendships and may utilize a variety of strategies for doing so. Because of their geographical mobility and its impact on their previous pattern of sociability, they are likely to have a greater need in their lives for new ties. Some organizations have developed means of integrating newcomers sociably. Think here of the ways colleges arrange their first few weeks to facilitate the development of friendships through encouraging the mixing of new students. Similarly, work organizations which regularly require mobility of their employees may instigate means of ensuring that new arrivals, and often their families, have opportunities to meet other employees working in the same area. A good example is the way the armed forces have developed means of integrating new arrivals through the informal rituals of the mess, welcoming committees, and other such mechanisms.

Finally, it is worth recognizing the impact that existing friendships can collectively have on one another. Here what matters is not that some new friendships are developed through existing friends, but more that there can be network consequences of different friendship patterns. For instance, where a group of people are all friends and form a cohesive group, each individual friendship gets reinforcement through the impact of the others. Each individual friendship will to some degree be patterned by the wider set of friendships of which it is part. Conversely, where two separate friends do not like each other, this will have an impact on the development of each relationship. Often the strain of trying to keep both relationships balanced will result in one being allowed to fade, tacitly if not through design. This, after all, is what often happens with divorce. Friends often start off not wanting to take sides, but in the end find remaining evenly balanced extremely difficult.

This section has looked at just four of the areas that shape people's 'immediate social environment' and consequently the 'space' there is in their lives for friendship and other equivalent sociable ties. There are of course many other facets of their lives which impinge more or less directly on friendship behaviour. The point has not been to provide an exhaustive list of these influences, but rather to indicate that friendship is not solely a matter of personality or, for that matter, of free will. Friendship, like kinship, may be informal but nonetheless it is patterned and shaped by a wide range of external influences, none of which are themselves crucial but all of which contour the ways in which friendships are organized. Thus in this sense, friendships need to be viewed as more than just personal relationships. They are also social, being one element within a wider social and economic constellation. The next section is also concerned with friendship as a social tie, but approaches this from a slightly different perspective, looking at the part that friendship plays within the wider social fabric.

Friendship in social life

Earlier it was pointed out that the study of friendship has not, in the main, been very sociological. The focus in much research has been on friendship as it affects the individual rather than on the wider role which friendship plays in social life. Thus studies have looked at the number of friends an individual has, at how those friendships are organized, and at how such matters relate to, say, personality attributes. What has received less attention are the ways in which friendship contributes to social life at a more general level (though see Litwak, 1985, 1989). Thus, there are few studies which examine the use to which friendships are put — for example, at how friendships help people cope with the demands of daily living, or with the crises they face, or how friendships are drawn on to further people's material interests.

Of course not all friendships are equivalent in their organization or significance. But it is important here to recognize that the concern should not be solely with 'best' or 'closest' friendships, nor even only with those relationships labelled as 'friendships'. What matters more is how the range of different relationships in an individual's 'sociability network' is used within social life. These relationships will, of course, differ. They will be activated in different contexts, have different exchange bases, involve different feelings of closeness and intimacy, and have different 'boundaries' constructed around them. Each friend will have access to different personal and social resources, have their own different needs and different responsibilities, and in the language used earlier, different 'space' available for friendship. But given these differences, questions can be posed about the role that friendship plays within the social fabric, about how friendship contributes to social life, and about the ways in which friendship ties in with other aspects of social organization (Litwak, 1985, 1989).

To examine these issues, it is useful to separate out four generic types of activity which are common elements within different types of friendship. These are: *sociability*; *practical support*; *emotional support*; and *confirmation of identity*. Clearly not all these elements will play an equal part in every friendship. Indeed, they will not all be present in every tie. However, in a simple fashion, they do represent some of the main ways in which different types of friendship contribute to social life (Allan, 1989; Wellman, 1992). Each will be discussed in turn below.

Sociability

The role of friends in sociability needs little commenting on. It is the most obvious basis of friendship and the route through which most friendships develop. Spending time with friends, taking part in activities with them, and discussing whatever issues are shared in common are the cornerstones of most friendships. Such routine interaction provides, amongst other things, a distraction from more serious aspects of life, a sense of social involvement, and a means of expressing elements of one's individuality and character. Most of the time people take these aspects of friendship for granted and reflect on them rather little. However, their significance is most apparent in their absence. That is, as studies of unemployment and of those who are housebound have shown, their value is recognized most when opportunities for engaging in a routine way with friends become restricted (Hobson, 1978; McKee and Bell, 1986; Gallie *et al.*, 1994).

Sociability can of course take many forms. In some relationships, shared social activities — hobbies and joint pastimes, visits to restaurants or pubs, sporting events, and so forth — provide the main frame of reference. In others, the emphasis is more directly on companionship and intimacy — talking, visiting each other, sharing news and gossip — rather than on specific activities. Of course, most friendships actually involve elements of both of these. Yet however the friendship is framed, whatever the activities that have come over time to define it and set the boundaries around what is considered the core of it, participation in friendship normally entails companionship and sociability, which is personally satisfying as well as being socially integrative (Jerrome, 1992).

Practical support

The role of friends in providing practical support is often underestimated, perhaps because it appears so mundane and obvious. However, along with the help provided by kin, it can play an important part in allowing people to achieve their personal projects and cope with the different demands made on them. The type of practical support friends provide varies widely, depending on each person's situation. Such things as giving friends lifts, returning library books for them, looking after their children, helping them to fix the car, taping music for them, and so forth are the bread and butter of friendship. Different friends will be drawn on in different ways depending on their skills and resources, as well as on the availability and circumstances of others, especially kin. The main point is that there is nothing unusual about drawing on — using — friends for practical support. They are a valuable resource, providing a means for us to negotiate our way through the various minor contingencies we face (Litwak, 1985; Willmott, 1987). This is well captured by Barry Wellman, who has described the services and help friends provide as 'much more than symbolic expressions of friendship'. They represent 'a wide range of flexible, low monetary cost, trustworthy, and efficient resources for domestic and paid work' (Wellman, 1985: 169).

The flexibility of the help that friends can provide is important, as is

---

Activity 8.1 Friendship and Favours

Think here of the favours you have done for friends over the last few days. Think too of the favours you have received. How have these helped you achieve your goals? What have they saved you from doing? How have you drawn on your friends? What role do they play in your daily routines?

---

the low-cost element. Often such flexibility is required if we are to meet the conflicting demands made of us by the relatively inflexible bureaucracies which dominate much social and economic life. This is not just at times of crisis, though the emotional and practical support friends can provide in such periods can be invaluable. Practical support is also valuable at more mundane times. Thus, achieving work objectives often depends on being able to call on colleagues and workmates informally to do small favours for us; friends can often help us meet the demands schools and colleges place on us, for example, allowing us to copy notes, providing help with homework, making excuses for us. Many other examples could be given from run-of-the-mill activities. The point is that friends do commonly act as a resource; people routinely draw on them to achieve their varied, mundane objectives.

Who we turn to for help depends very much on contextual and situational factors: the help needed; the particular circumstances at hand; who is available; the exchange basis of the relationship; the different character and skills a person has. While most of us draw most heavily on a few friends, we are usually careful about not asking too much of any one. What counts as 'too much', though, itself varies. As discussed in the last chapter, what matters is the degree of reciprocity that can be maintained. It is generally important that friendships do not get out of balance, so usually part of the consideration of asking friends to help is whether there is some way in which we can repay them. By and large, with most friendships though not all, this means that the help that we ask for is usually quite limited. In this way reciprocation is less problematic so that the balance of the tie can be protected. There is then less danger of us being seen as 'abusing' the friendship.

Generally, for more major assistance we turn to primary kin, for as we saw in earlier chapters these ties are more enduring and less dependent on the need for reciprocity and balance. But while the practical support received from friends is often mundane and relatively minor, this does not mean that it is socially or, indeed, personally insignificant. As noted, its importance is that it does provide people with an accessible, reliable, and cheap means of managing the day-to-day contingencies they face. Without these informal relationships acting as a resource which people can draw on in a flexible fashion, fulfilling their goals and meeting the demands made on them would become much more onerous. Thus the practical role which informal relationships play in people's negotiation of their way through the routines of everyday life should not be underestimated.

Emotional support

As well as practical support, friends regularly provide each other with emotional support of various forms. This may simply consist of talking over issues in people's lives of a minor or more major sort that are currently causing them concern — a child's behaviour, a difficulty at work, how to cope with conflicting demands, or whatever. As with practical help, who is talked to about what issues will depend on the way specific relationships are framed and the matter causing concern. Some topics will not be considered relevant to some relationships. This may be because of the degree of intimacy concerned, because the other person is deemed to have little knowledge of the particular issue, or because the topic is defined as outside the bounds of the friendship. Thus friends at work may be used mainly to discuss work issues, but drawn on less for advice about family dilemmas, though here the gender issues discussed in the last chapter are probably important. (See also Marks, 1994.)

Discussion of relatively mundane matters currently causing concern is part and parcel of many friendships. Through discussion of such issues, solidarity between the friends develops, the identity of the friends as individuals is cemented, and moral support provided. But, of course, not all the problems we face in life are mundane or minor. Some are of major concern and may be regarded as confidential and private, such as crises within a marriage, issues of illness or death, or difficulties with family or other relationships. People often limit who they confide in over such issues, choosing only their closest, most trusted friends (Oliker, 1989). Here the support given is likely to be much more one-sided than that occurring in the routine discussion of hassles and irritations common to many sociable ties. Because of this imbalance, the established level of trust needs to be greater, especially if the issue is thought to reflect discreditably in some way on yourself or your family. At times, though, the process can act in reverse. Confiding in someone who has not previously been that close, for example, because they are known to have undergone a similar experience, can result in the development of a stronger bond. For some issues, such as divorce or marital violence, this may be an important means by which friendship networks gradually get modified in the way discussed in the previous chapter (Allan, 1989).

Confirmation of identity

The fourth aspect of friendship mentioned above was that of confirmation of identity. From the individual's perspective, it can be argued that social life consists of a series of roles, many of which, though by no means all, are played out against the background of formal organizations of different sorts. A good deal of an individual's social identity is derived directly or otherwise from the social roles they occupy: student; mother; dentist; teacher; whatever. And yet clearly each individual is more than these roles, is more than the sum of these social parts. There is also the person as a person, with their own peculiar habits, their own little ways which together with the role performances make up our recognized identity. Such identities are of course not fixed. They change as our roles change, and as we develop new facets of self over time.

Now friendships can be significant in the integration of these different elements of self. To begin with, friends often play an important part in moulding, reinforcing and, on occasion, challenging each other's identities. They do so in a variety of ways, some more subtle than others. As noted above, one way is through the emotional and moral support they offer. So too they can do so through jokes and ribbing, not allowing one another to have too many pretensions or to make unjustified claims for the self. The use of humour in friendship as a form of social control represents a non-threatening means of establishing the boundaries of self-identity. But mainly friends confirm each other's identities through their normal, unexceptional interactions. The topics they discuss; the debates they have; the perceptions of the world they portray; their recounting of past events or current adventures; the gossip they engage in; all these mundane activities common to all friendships serve to establish and reinforce the individual's social identity (Hess, 1972; Rubin, 1985; Jerrome, 1992).

The emphasis on equality within friendship also plays a part in affirming social identity. Friends are people who are perceived as essentially 'like us'. In terms of the old proverb: 'Birds of a feather flock together.' Thus through association, we define ourselves. But there is more to it than this. Remember the arguments made in the last chapter about the ways in which friendships alter as our social position or social status changes. Quite typically, old friends whose social identity is dissimilar to ours are slowly shed and replaced by others whose identity is more consonant with our new status. What is happening here? It is more than just replacing as friends people with whom it is now harder to maintain an easy balance of exchange. What is also happening in these shifts in friendship networks is that support is being generated for the individual's new social identity.

Consider a specific example, that of women returning to study at university after having left school early. Frequently these women return to education with the support of their friends and families (Suitor, 1987). When they first enter university life, they are typically unsure of themselves, uncertain of their right to be reading for a degree, and think that they are likely to fail. As time progresses and they achieve satisfactory grades, so too their commitment to university life becomes greater. Increasingly, achieving high grades becomes important to them, as does exploring new ideas. In a very clear sense they have made the transition to 'student', not just in that this is now one of their major roles, but rather in the sense that this is now part of their identity, part of the way they define themselves as people.

But as they become more committed to academic achievement, so in many ways they become more distant from their previous friends. Often their new knowledge may drive a wedge between them; certainly their passion for academic work at the expense of other activities makes others believe they have 'changed', that they are no longer as compatible or as supportive as they were. Others do not see why they wish to stay up till late in the night reading texts, nor do they fully appreciate the importance of achieving high grades. As a result, there is often a reduced involvement with these friends, and a greater involvement with other mature students studying similar subjects. With these people they share their enthusiasms and their new identities. They receive support for their academic effort and an appreciation of why these things matter.

The role of friends in affirming and cementing people's social identities is clear in this example. Now just as this happens with students returning to study, so too it happens with other status transitions, including those of marriage, divorce, promotions at work, and the like. But importantly, similar processes occur when there has been no status change at all, though often this is much harder to recognize. As we have seen, one of the ways friends provide each other with a sense of identity is by recognizing each person's individuality, independently of the more formal role positions each happens to hold. Yet at the same time, it seems friends rarely undermine those role positions very extensively. Rather, they tend far more to provide support for them and confirm their significance for the individual. There is, in other words, a degree of articulation between the roles people play and the identities their friends endorse (Jerrome, 1984; Oliker, 1989).

On the one hand, friendship provides a social forum in which external role performance appears to be of little consequence — it is the individual that matters, not their role performance outside the friendship. Yet, on the other, the friendships themselves are often built around and cement the importance of these roles in people's lives. At times, of course, tension may emerge between one's role positions and the activities undertaken with particular friends, but by and large this is rare. More usually, friendships act as counterpoints to other roles, but do not threaten their performance.

A good example is provided by Jerrome (1984) in her study of middle-aged, middle-class women. She shows very clearly that while the women she studied complained about their husbands and families to one another, the activities they engaged in — quite extensive entertaining, for example, with an emphasis on appearance and style — confirmed their commitment to a particular form of femininity and a relatively conservative view of domestic life. Thus their friendships allowed them to express their individuality without undermining their identity as successful and accomplished middle-class women. Exactly the same processes of friendships acting in support of identities framed by people's wider location within the social realm occur in most friendships.

Conclusion

This chapter has explored some of the ways in which friendship is linked to broader social and economic factors. As noted earlier, sociable ties, such as friendship, are often viewed as essentially personal, as ties which are matters of individual choosing and volition. Who people have as friends, how much time they spend with them, what they do together, are, in this light, taken to be issues which are not influenced very heavily by external considerations. From a sociological angle, however, friendship can be seen to be rather more than this. As the first part of this chapter discussed, friendships are not free-standing relationships; they are not created or sustained in a social or economic void. Rather, what can be conceived of as each individual's immediate social environment has a definite influence on the overall organization of their friendships. Just as personality matters, so too the constellation of interests and commitments each person has will shape the pattern of their friendships.

So too, as discussed in the later part of the chapter, friendships are of social as well as personal consequence. Friendship is not a social luxury. Within modern society, friendship, along with other forms of personal relationship including a number of kin ties, provides people with practical and emotional support, as well as playing a part in the construction of their personal identities. Just as important, friendships help integrate people into the social realm and act as a resource for managing some of the mundane and exceptional events which confront them in their lives. There is a limit to which any particular friendship is drawn on for support, not least because of the need for reciprocity and balance. However, to cite Jerrome's phrase again, the role of friends in cementing together 'the bricks of social structure' (1984: 715) is important.

Further reading

The books mentioned as further reading in the last chapter are also relevant for this one. In addition, *Friendship: Developing a Sociological Perspective* (1989) by Graham Allan examines the issues raised in this chapter more fully. Though both Peter Nardi's collection *Men's Friendships* (1992) and Stacey Oliker's *Best Friends and Marriage* (1989) are written from an American angle, they include plenty of material which is relevant to the themes of this chapter.

Chapter Nine

Conclusion: Social Networks and Informal Ties

Most of this book has been concerned with examining the character of kinship and friendship as separate types of relationship. In many ways this is sensible, because kinship and friendship are based on different principles and do occupy different social realms. Yet at another level, treating kin ties and friend ties as totally discrete and separate is itself questionable. Without getting into issues of the extent to which kin and friend relationships can be substituted for one another, it does seem worth while considering informal relationships in unison if we are to understand their role in modern society. That is, without ignoring the significant differences there are between various categories of relationship, a sociology of informal relationships needs to take a more global perspective than one which treats each form of relationship individually (Morgan, 1975; Allan, 1979).

There have been various attempts to do this. The theoretical perspectives discussed in Chapter 2 are amongst the most influential. In particular, those theories that claimed a decline in communal and familial solidarity had a vision of the ways in which industrialization had altered the significance of informal relationships in social life. Yet the empirical evidence, both contemporary and historical, relevant to these theories is not entirely persuasive. We know primary kin ties remain significant to people, both in practical and emotional terms, even if they are not as central in the organization of daily life as they once were. And we know that friendships are important for people too, again in terms of both practical support and emotional meaning. Virtually all the studies which have focused on these issues, in Britain and in the United States, have come to the same general conclusions.

And yet clearly it would be curious if the role of informal relationships in everyday life did not alter as the economic and social bases of society were transformed with the development of modernity in its different

115

guises. Industrialization affected every facet of life; it inevitably altered kinship and other informal relationships. So too, the changes occurring more recently with the emergence of what Giddens (1991) terms 'late modernity' have also had an impact on the social organization of informal ties. A major premiss of this book has been that informal relationships, be they ties of kinship or friendship, often have the appearance of being removed and separate from the main business of social and economic life but in reality are integral to it. If this is so, then it obviously follows that such relationships will be modified as the social and economic structure of society is transformed. This insight lies at the heart of a sociological appreciation of informal relationships.

In this chapter, then, the aim is to look at informal relationships generally and consider how best the part they play in contemporary life can be understood. In doing this, the chapter will draw on an approach which has been referred to in various chapters but not developed in any depth. This is the approach known as social network analysis. Although the idea of social networks was originally developed in Britain, there have been relatively few studies in this country which have utilized the approach in a full fashion for examining people's informal relationships. Consequently this chapter will rely for much of its material on research carried out in North America. Having discussed the potential of a social network perspective, the chapter will conclude by revisiting the discussion of privatization developed in Chapter 2.

Social network analysis

Network analysis gained popularity in sociology through the work of two British social anthropologists, John Barnes and Elizabeth Bott. Barnes introduced the idea of examining informal relationships in terms of a network in reporting on a study of a small fishing village in Norway (Barnes, 1954). In the course of his fieldwork, he realized that what held social life together was what he later called 'the ever-ramifying web of cognatic kinship, affinity and friendship' (Barnes, 1969: 72). In more simple language, what needed to be understood was the ways in which informal relationships were used by members of the village to achieve their aims and to provide a framework of order.

Appropriately enough for a study of a fishing village, this led Barnes to think of informal relationships as a net. The lines of the net were the individual relationships which people maintained, while the places where the lines joined one another — the nodes in the net — were the individuals involved. Thus the network provided a visual analogy of the total set of informal ties maintained in the village, each link within the network representing a different relationship. This idea of representing informal relationships as a net attracted wide attention and was developed further by Elizabeth Bott in her study of twenty London families, *Family and Social Networks* (1957; 2nd edn. 1971), one of the most influential studies of family issues ever produced. What Bott did as the result of extensive informal interviews with these families was plot out the networks which each family maintained, based on who they knew, and on the relationships these others maintained independently with one another.

On the basis of the analysis of these networks, Bott argued that there was a link between the structure of the networks married couples maintained and the organization of their domestic lives. Specifically, she hypothesized that the 'degree of segregation in the role-relationship of husband and wife varies directly with the connectedness of the family's social network' (Bott, 1971: 60). Whether or not Bott's analysis is correct (and there has been much research and debate generated by it; see Milardo and Allan, 1996 for a review) is not really relevant here. What matters is the impact it had on the use of a network approach for understanding the significance of the set of informal ties in which individuals were embedded. More than any other study, Bott's opened up the way for fresh appreciations of the part such relationships played in shaping people's lives.

There were a number of reasons why Bott's work attracted so much attention. Two are particularly relevant here. First, it appeared to offer a solution to the vexed question of 'community'. In contrast to the definitional wrangles and the normative assumptions which the idea of community contained, network analysis offered a far more rigorous way of recording the patterns of informal relationships which actually existed. It allowed the set of relationships to which individuals were party to be laid out in diagrammatic form, and in turn this mapping allowed a far fuller appreciation of the interconnections involved. In addition, unlike traditional notions of 'community', network analysis was not restricted to relationships which occurred in the same locality. It could readily incorporate all informal relationships irrespective of whether they were local. This was important given the reduced significance of the 'local' in most people's lives with the development of mass transport and communication systems.

Second, network analysis attracted much support because, at least in the way Bott had used it, it offered the prospect of explaining social actions in a form which was anything but trivial. If the connectedness (or density as it later became known) of people's social networks was strongly linked to marital organization, then in theory at least network configuration might also help to explain a range of other social activities. Thus the idea of network became much more than a metaphor or even a mode of description. With the publication of Bott's study, it had become, in Barnes's later phrase, an 'orienting statement' with a central theme that 'the configuration of cross-cutting inter-personal bonds is in some unspecified way causally connected with the actions of these persons and with the social institutions of their society' (1972: 2). The details would need to be specified, but the promise that network analysis held out to those interested in community and informal relationships was apparent.

In fact, it is questionable whether this particular promise has really been fulfilled with regard to community sociology. Bott's results have not been replicated despite a number of attempts to do so, and other causal explanations of a similar character to hers have not been advanced, at least not in so elegant a form (Milardo and Allan, 1996). At the same time, though, there has been an explosion of interest in network analysis among sociologists of different sorts. (See Wellman and Berkowitz, 1988, and Scott, 1991 for reviews.) Here we will only consider those approaches which are directly concerned with examining the field of personal relationships. As we will see, the language of network has become common currency, but quite frequently the concepts have been used in a fashion that makes the approach appear less innovative and less satisfactory.

Personal networks and personal stars

In order to understand the direction that network analysis has taken in this field, it is first necessary to understand what exactly networks are. As Figure 9.1 illustrates, the initial conception of social networks was that they would be full depictions of not only the individuals known to a person (or as in Bott's research, a couple), but also of the relationships there were between these others. Methodologically, collecting such information is an extremely complex (and expensive) task, except where you are only interested in a relatively small group, like that found, for instance, in a particular workplace or other bounded social setting. To do it properly would involve collecting data from person A about their contacts and then interviewing the other people mentioned about the people they know to see if the others named by person A are

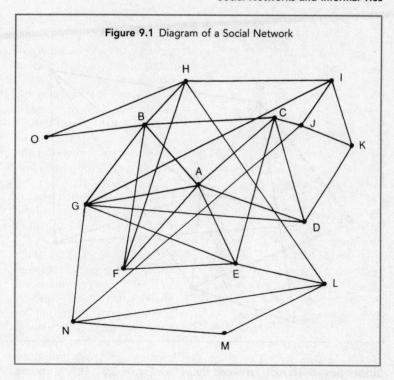

Figure 9.1 Diagram of a Social Network

also directly linked to the other interviewees. Indeed, one could extend this further by then going on to interview the people identified by interviewees B, C, D, etc. to see what relationships they maintain. This could be continued *ad infinitum*, and of course would need to be if a genuinely full network were to be collected. This, though, is obviously impractical.

Instead of doing this, most researchers have merely asked their respondents about those they know, sometimes without gathering additional information about the further relationships between those named. Thus in Barnes's terms, the information being collected is at best about personal (or 'ego-centred') networks or just personal stars. As illustrated in Figure 9.2, a personal network is essentially one in which data are limited to the relationships between the known contacts of a given individual (usually the respondent), while a personal star consists solely of those others an individual knows, irrespective of any

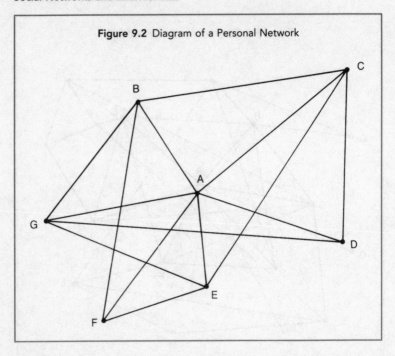

Figure 9.2 Diagram of a Personal Network

further ties which exist between them (see Figure 9.3). This of course simplifies data collection but does generate a different level of information than proponents of a network perspective first envisaged. There is another problem here too. It is that quite often researchers who want to ensure that they have a reasonably representative (and therefore usually quite large) sample of respondents are forced, because of cost factors, to limit the range of relationships about which they can ask their respondents for information. Thus they might, for example, only ask people about their four or six closest or most frequently seen contacts outside the household.

A further difficulty with constructing social networks lies in deciding which relationships should be included. Bott's original formulation was deceptively simple: it relied on specifying all those known to her respondents. But what exactly do we mean here by 'known'? Various people have tried to estimate how many others people on average know. The numbers estimated are surprisingly large, in the range of 1,000 to 1,500 (Boissevain, 1974; Pool and Kochen, 1978). While contemporary computers may have the power to deal with these sorts of

Figure 9.3 Diagram of a Personal Star

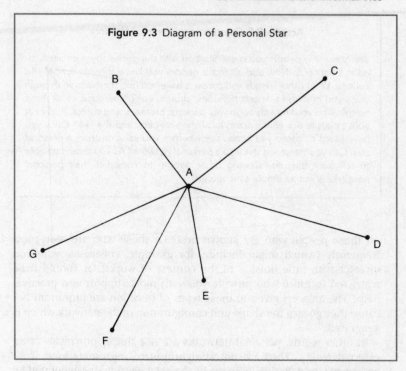

number, ascertaining information about the relationships maintained with all these people, and then with all the other 1,000 to 1,500 others they all know, is some task.

Now if you try out Activity 9.1, it should be clear to you that at the boundaries you have to make decisions about who you 'know'. There are some people who you have met and who may recognize you but do not have anything very much to do with you or know anything about you. These are, in a sense, equivalent to the kin who were un-named in Firth's characterization discussed in Chapter 4. This issue is actually more significant than it first appears. Just as you have to decide which people to include and which to exclude, so too the same applies to any construction of social networks. Some relationships are sufficiently significant to warrant inclusion while others are deemed to be of lesser consequence. But on what criteria should it be decided to include people? And how does the decision about criteria relate to the theoretical concerns which drive the network analysis in the first place? For example, should the collection of network members concentrate

---

Activity 9.1 Constructing a Personal Network

See how many people you know. Start off with the genealogy you constructed in Chapter 3. Now add all those people you know through school and
college. What other friends and contacts have you got, for example through
clubs you belong to, sports activities, church, etc.? Now think of all those
people who you know through your parents, brothers, and sisters. And what
about people like your doctor, local shopkeepers, and the like? Once you
have listed all those you know, see whether you can construct a personal
star. Can you transform this into a personal network? As you should be able
to tell from this, interviewing other people to construct their personal
networks is not as simple as it sounds!

---

on those people who are known best? Or those who are seen most
frequently (which might include, for example, colleagues who you
interact with little outside of the context of work)? Or should it be
restricted to those who provide you with most support and practical
help? The answers given to these types of question are important because they govern the shape and configuration of the network which is
generated.

In other words, personal networks are not simply portrayals of an
external reality. They are not straightforward representations of an
empirical world. Rather, they are analytical constructions generated by
the researcher, which certainly aim to reflect the real circumstances of
respondents but which nonetheless operate with an analytical filter.
That is, the network which is constructed by the researcher reflects the
criteria which she or he chose about which ties should be included and
which should not. Thus, and this is the important point, the shape or
configuration of the network is actually a consequence of these analytical decisions. In other words, the configurational properties of a personal (or any other sort of) network, which are those characteristics like
network density which network analysts focus on, are not fixed but
depend on what the analyst takes to constitute a link. As Mitchell emphasized a good while ago, 'any statement we may wish to make about
the morphological features of a social network must be premised upon
what links constituting the framework of the network are assumed to
be' (1974: 22).

In recent years the significance of this has been recognized more
widely and efforts have been made to specify more tightly the different

dimensions of network links. Milardo (1992), for instance, has recently distinguished between two different personal networks based on separate criteria for the inclusion of relationships. The first of these he terms 'psychological networks'. These are composed of people who the respondent considers important or significant in their lives. In terms of the kinship categories discussed in Chapter 4, they are closest to the intimate kin set. These people have developed strong relationships with the individual over time but, depending on circumstances, may not now be interacted with very frequently. The second type of network Milardo delineates is 'interactive networks'. These consist of people with whom there is frequent interaction — family, colleagues, friends — and with whom we exchange advice, support, and aid. Note how even here the boundary problem remains: how much advice or whatever do we need to exchange to warrant including the other person in the network? While this and other classifications help bring greater rigour to network construction, remember that the networks created remain analytical constructions, and consequently so too are the network properties they embody (Scott, 1991).

The use of personal networks

As discussed earlier, Bott (1971) attempted to use network properties, in particular network density, to explain marital organization. In more recent work, the emphasis on explanation has not been so pronounced. Instead, what researchers have concentrated on rather more is using network approaches as a means of depicting people's social worlds, that is, the overall sets of informal relationships in which they are involved. What this allows is for comparison to be made between the personal networks which people with different social and economic characteristics have, and also for changes in people's networks to be plotted as their own personal circumstances change.

One of the most important contributions to personal-network analysis has been made by Barry Wellman in his studies of informal relationships in East York, Toronto (Wellman, 1979, 1985, 1992; Wellman et al., 1988; Wellman and Wortley, 1990). Wellman's aim was to examine whether it was true that people had become more isolated and less involved in local social relationships in the manner suggested by 'loss of community' theories. He initially undertook a large-scale survey of over 800 residents of East York. As with other large-scale studies, he asked each respondent about a relatively small number — in his case, six — of their most significant relationships instead of trying to plot their full personal networks (Wellman, 1979). The results of the survey showed that while the locality was a source of few close relationships, people were not as a consequence socially isolated. The majority did maintain significant personal relationships, both with kin and non-kin, but not in most instances with others living nearby. Modern technologies, in particular cars and phones, allowed these non-local relationships to be kept alive without much difficulty.

Yet while this survey, like others of its kind, provided useful data on the major personal relationships of those involved, and in particular, data that demonstrated the weakness of some theorizing about the nature of community in the later twentieth century, it also became evident that the shallowness of the material gathered in this sort of large-scale survey limited the understanding of the networks that could develop. As a result, Wellman extended his study by conducting far more extensive research on a subsample of 33 of the original respondents ten years later (Wellman *et al.*, 1988). While this is a very small number from which to generalize about contemporary personal networks, it did allow information on the relationships people maintained to be examined in far greater depth. As a result of this Wellman has been able to add considerably to our knowledge of how personal networks differ and what types of factor influence these differences.

Wellman's 33 respondents reported over 400 'significant' ties, that is 'relationships they actively think about and maintain (although not necessarily through frequent contact)' (ibid. 137). These included 164 'intimate' relationships, which were ones identified by the respondents as socially close, and 96 'routine' ties, in which there was contact, in person or by phone, at least 3 times a week. On average the respondents in this study had at least 11 active ties in their personal networks. Most had at least 4 intimate contacts and 3 people with whom they were in contact 3 or more times a week (ibid. 140).

Only 4 of the 33 respondents were judged to be socially isolated, 2 having fewer than 6 members in their active networks. In contrast, 9 had more than 20 significant members in their networks. For all but one person, immediate kin were important others, making up almost half of all active and intimate ties. The other significant members of these people's personal networks consisted in the main of a combination of friends, co-workers, and, especially for women, neighbours. The ties themselves had lasted a surprisingly long time. Their average duration was 19 years, though clearly this is a consequence of the inclusion of kin as part of their active networks. However, Wellman *et al.* reported that even the non-kin relationships had lasted for 8 years on average (ibid. 146).

So it is clear that most of the respondents in this study were not socially isolated. They maintained a range of informal relationships that were important to them, in terms of both personal attachment and mundane support. Aside from the kinship links though, the networks in which people were incorporated tended not to have particularly high densities. That is, the close friends which the respondents had did not necessarily know one another particularly well. Collectively these ties provided Wellman's respondents with a good deal of support, even though the tendency was for individual ties to be restricted to specific types of help. As Wellman *et al.* (ibid. 174–5) note, the various informal relationships their respondents maintained provided them with '*havens*: a sense of being wanted and belonging, and readily available companionship..."*band-aids*": emotional aid and small services... *ladders* to change their situations... and *levers*... to change the world'. These ties 'are important to the routine operations of households, crucial to the management of crises, and sometimes instrumental in helping respondents change their situations' (Wellman and Wortley, 1990: 583; Wellman, 1992).

In ways like this, thinking of the various relationships which people maintain within their personal network can help generate a fuller understanding of the part that informal ties play in everyday life. Certainly the language of network has had a big impact on the way in which these relationships are conceptualized and reported. Indeed, it is noticeable in Britain how this approach has now become common currency. In particular, those concerned with analysing the care provided to people, especially elderly people in need of support, often write about 'networks of carers', though they rarely explore the full meanings of this notion. On the other hand, some studies have tried to understand patterns of care provision through looking systematically at the different personal-care networks available to elderly people.

Wenger's longitudinal study of the support received by elderly people in rural north Wales (1984, 1989, 1995) is particularly important. Wenger found that on average her elderly respondents had between five and seven members in their *support* networks, i.e. not their overall personal networks but those people available to provide care and support on a regular basis. This figure is in line with that found elsewhere (Wenger, 1989). As might be expected from the research discussed in Chapter 6, the majority of the people in the support network were kin. Like Wellman, Wenger first conducted a large-scale survey investigating the supportive relationships maintained by a sample of elderly people

(Wenger, 1984). She then followed this up with a far more intensive, three-year study of 30 of the respondents aged 75 or over included in the first phase (Wenger, 1989). She has also been involved in other studies of the support networks of older people (Wenger, 1995).

However, Wenger took a different stance to Wellman and his colleagues in analysing the support networks. Rather than examining the configurational properties like density or clique structure, she focused on the variation there was in overall network composition. She was able to identify five different types of network based on three criteria: (1) the availability of close kin; (2) the level of involvement of family, friends, and neighbours; and (3) the level of interaction with voluntary and community groups (Wenger, 1989, 1995: 61–2). The five types were:

1. *the local family-dependent support network*: mainly relying on close kin, who often shared a household or lived locally;
2. *the locally integrated support network*: typically consisting of local family, friends, and neighbours;
3. *the local self-contained support network*: usually restricted in scale and containing mainly neighbours, with comparatively little kin involvement;
4. *the wider community-focused support network*: typically involving a high level of community activities, and a high number of friends and kin;
5. *the private restricted support network*: characterized by an absence of close kin, aside from a spouse in some cases, and with few friends or neighbours.

The commonest form of support network appears to be the locally integrated one, followed by the local family-dependent one. Interestingly, these two were also the most 'robust' in terms of providing elderly people with informal support. The particular form which support networks take is influenced by factors like the size of the individual's primary kin group, her or his level of geographical mobility, and her or his class position (Wenger, 1995).

Networks: kinship and other ties

There can be no doubt that the concept of network has come to play a significant part in the study of informal relationships. Rather than just focusing on one type of tie — say, kinship, or neighbourship, or friendship — it provides a framework for appreciating the interplay of all these different relationships. Moreover this framework is structural. Instead of simply allowing the characteristics of individual relationships to be assessed and compared, it allows for comparisons to be made between some of the collective properties of the set of relationships any individual (or family or other social unit) maintains. While this is generally in terms of the configurational patterns within a network, subtlety can be added by making the network models more complex and differentiating within them relationships which have different qualities. This certainly allows for comparisons to be made quite readily between different people, between the types of relationships people are committed to at different times, and between the dominant forms of networks in different societies.

Whether or not this framework of itself generates explanations of social action in the Bott form can be left aside for now. What matters is that the approach has opened up new and interesting questions about personal ties, replacing older formulations which, if not redundant, appeared at the time to be offering few new insights. At the same time, it is worth recognizing that the network approach does not offer all the answers. Examining the part which different personal relationships play in people's lives is a crucial task within the sociology of kinship and other personal ties. There is much to be gained from seeing kinship as part of a wider set of ties (Allan, 1979). Yet network perspectives are just that: perspectives, ways of seeing and interpreting some of the patterns which occur. They cannot provide a complete picture. Other types of question which the approach is less well equipped to answer are also important.

Thus social network analysis cannot fully answer questions about the sense of obligation and commitment we feel towards particular ties, even though it can indicate some of the ways in which we are embedded in cliques or highly dense sets of relationships and so constrained by the costs to our other relationships of behaving in ways defined as inappropriate in any one. Equally, network analysis cannot of itself explain why some friendships matter more than others, why kinship plays a larger part in some people's lives than in other people's, or indeed often why we construct the particular social networks we do. It allows us to see these patterns more clearly, but it does not explain them solely in its own terms.

Yet this is no mean achievement. Done properly, and one can argue that certainly in Britain but also elsewhere few have managed to collect data on personal networks with the same thoroughness as Bott back in the 1950s, the relative significance of different personal relationships in people's lives can be appreciated more fully. The great achievement of social network analysis for the study of personal relationships is that it encourages a rigour in the conceptualization of research problems that is often missing in other perspectives and also provides a framework for the systematic collection of information. It may not have generated in full the explanatory advances once heralded, but it has certainly led to new and interesting questions being asked. In particular, the concepts of personal stars but, more significantly, personal networks have quietly revolutionized the ways in which people's informal relationships are thought about in sociology and social science more broadly.

Conclusion: Privatization and social networks

By way of conclusion, let us briefly return to some of the issues which were raised in Chapter 2, in particular those concerning the extent to which contemporary social life is becoming privatized. Leaving aside questions about social participation in the past, what we can recognize is that the idea of privatization contains in it a number of themes which are analytically distinct. Three are worth considering in this conclusion. They are, first, the idea that most people's social life does not revolve around communal sociability in public settings; second, the idea that the home and domestic relations are given priority over their other relationships; and third, the idea that people lead relatively isolated social lives. Let us consider each in turn.

From the different studies that have been discussed throughout this book, it is evident that the majority of sociability is not communal in the way simpler notions of the privatization thesis suggest it was in the past. Thus, for example, the neighbourhood is not significant as a source of social solidarity for the majority of people. Nor do most people interact with others principally in settings which are, in some sense, 'collective'. Certainly informal relationships are often developed and activated in 'public' or 'semi-public' settings, like social clubs, pubs, and other activity-based contexts. And equally, individuals can experience satisfaction from the solidarity which such collective settings encourage. However, for most people, such settings are places for developing and sustaining particular relationships with a few individual others, rather than being places of communal involvement *per se.* As noted in Chapter 7, there appear to be class and gender variations in the extent of this form of communal involvement, but overall the majority of personal networks contain strong individual ties rather than being more amorphously 'communal'.

Second, it can be recognized that the home and the domestic relationships entailed in it are highly significant for the majority of people throughout most life-course phases. As discussed in earlier chapters, marriage, children, and the construction of a satisfactory home life are high on the list of people's priorities. To this extent, social life in the late twentieth century can be described quite accurately as 'home-centred'. Within this, the home is used by many as a suitable location for socializing with others (Wellman, 1992). Primary kin relationships, in particular, are normally activated and serviced within the home. Indeed, familialism and domesticity are central concerns of these relationships. But for friends and other non-kin too, the home is often a key setting for sociability. A range of factors influence this, including in particular class position and marital organization. But generally, as people commit more resources to their home, so it appears the home becomes a place to which people can be invited rather than excluded (Franklin, 1989).

Finally, there is the question of whether people lead socially isolated lives. The answer to this should be clear. It is, of course, that most people do not. Most of us have personal networks which contain large numbers of others, and within which a smaller number are particularly important to us. Some of these important relationships are with kin and some are with non-kin. The patterns here do vary depending on a wide range of circumstances. And equally, some people do lead quite restricted lives and are socially isolated. The point, though, is that this is relatively unusual rather than the normal state of affairs in contemporary society. As we have seen in this chapter, even those elderly people who might be expected to be most isolated have active support networks with an average of five to seven members in them.

Yet in a sense Wellman is right to argue that the individual relationships to which people are party have themselves become 'privatized'. This, though, does not mean that life-styles under contemporary social and economic conditions are privatized in a fuller sense. What it means is, first, that sociable relationships are frequently enacted away from public gaze and scrutiny. This certainly applies to most primary kin ties. However, many friendships are also organized in this fashion, with the private sphere being one of the key arenas in which friends engage with each other. Second, it means that social networks overall often have lower densities than would otherwise be the case. Although the subset of kin ties within the personal network will be highly connected, friendships are often more individual. An individual's different friends are quite likely to have met each other through that individual, but they are not themselves necessarily friends or involved with each other in any other way. Thus these parts of the personal network will have relatively low densities.

Overall it can be recognized that social life under conditions of contemporary modernity is more complex than the idea of privatization initially implies. However, drawing on the idea of social and personal networks in the manner different analysts have is an extremely useful tool for capturing some of the variations which occur, though, as the earlier part of this chapter made clear, the concept of 'network' is not a panacea for all the problems of accurately representing the character of people's social participation and involvement. Nonetheless, the network approach does offer a useful aid for understanding and interpreting the range of informal relationships in which people are involved. Although adequate network studies are quite expensive to conduct, it would certainly be valuable to have more research, especially in Britain, which explored systematically the patterning of the social networks people maintain and the ways these change over time as their circumstances alter. It would then be possible to explore more fully the various ways in which social life is affected by changes in social and economic conditions.

Further reading

Analysing social networks quickly becomes technical. John Scott's *Social Network Analysis: A Handbook* (1991) provides a very clear introduction to the topic, though the treatment of the material in later chapters is necessarily quite advanced. *Social Structures: A Network Approach* (1988) by Barry Wellman and S. D. Berkowitz includes a number of chapters which explore the development and utility of network analysis for a range of issues in sociology, including those discussed in this chapter.

References

ADAMS, R. G. (1987), 'Patterns of network change: a longitudinal study of friendships of elderly women', *The Gerontologist*, 27: 222–7.

—— (1989), 'Conceptual and methodological issues in studying friendships of older adults', in Adams and Blieszner (eds.) (1989).

—— and BLIESZNER, R. (eds.) (1989), *Older Adult Friendships: Structure and Process*, Newbury Park, Sage.

ALLAN, G. (1979), *A Sociology of Friendship and Kinship*, London, Allen and Unwin.

—— (1982), 'Property and family solidarity', in Hollowell, P. (ed.), *Property and Social Relations*, London, Heinemann.

—— (1985), *Family Life: Domestic Roles and Social Organization*, Oxford, Blackwell.

—— (1986), 'Friendship and care for elderly people', *Ageing and Society*, 6: 1–12.

—— (1989), *Friendship: Developing a Sociological Perspective*, Hemel Hempstead, Harvester Wheatsheaf.

—— (1991), 'Social work, community care and informal networks', in Davies, M. (ed.), *The Sociology of Social Work*, London, Routledge.

—— and ADAMS, R. G. (1989), 'Aging and the structure of friendship', in Adams and Blieszner (eds.) (1989).

—— and CROW, G. (1991), 'Privatization, home-centredness and leisure', *Leisure Studies*, 10: 19–32.

ALLATT, P., and YEANDLE, S. (1991), *Youth Unemployment and the Family: Voices of Disordered Times*, London, Routledge.

ANDERSON, M. (1971), *Family Structure in Nineteenth Century Lancashire*, Cambridge, Cambridge University Press.

ARBER, S., and GILBERT, N. (1989), 'Men: the forgotten carers', *Sociology*, 23: 111–18.

—— and GINN, J. (1992), ' "In sickness and in health": care-giving, gender and the independence of elderly people', in Marsh, C., and Arber, S. (eds.), *Families and Households: Divisions and Change*, London, Macmillan.

ARENSBERG, C., and KIMBALL, S. (1940), *Family and Community in Ireland*, London, Peter Smith.

BALLARD, R. (ed.) (1994), *Desh Pardesh: The South Asian Presence in Britain*, London, Hurst.

BANKOFF, E. (1981), 'Effects of friendship support on the psychological well-being of widows', in Lopata, H. Z., and Maines, D. (eds.), *Research in the Interweave of Social Roles: Friendship*, Greenwich, Conn., Jai Press.

BARCLAY REPORT (1982), *Social Workers: Their Role and Tasks*, London, Bedford Square Press.

BARNES, J. A. (1954), 'Class and committees in a Norwegian island parish', *Human Relations*, 7: 39–58.

References

BARNES, J. A. (1969), 'Networks and political process', in Mitchell, J. C. (ed.), *Social Networks in Urban Situations*, Manchester, Manchester University Press.

—— (1972), 'Social Networks', *Module in Anthropology*, No. 26, Reading, Mass., Addison-Wesley.

BELL, C. (1968), *Middle Class Families*, London, Routledge and Kegan Paul.

BELL, R. (1981), *Worlds of Friendship*, Beverly Hills, Calif., Sage.

BHACHU, P. (1985), *Twice Migrants: East African Sikh Settlers in Britain*, London, Tavistock.

BINNS, D., and MARS, G. (1984), 'Family, community and unemployment: a study in change', *Sociological Review*, 32: 662–95.

BLAU, Z. (1961), 'Structural constraints on friendship in old age', *American Sociological Review*, 26: 429–39.

BLIESZNER, R., and ADAMS, R. G. (1992), *Adult Friendship*, Newbury Park, Sage.

BOISSEVAIN, J. (1974), *Friends of Friends*, Oxford, Blackwell.

BOTT, E. (1957, 2nd edn. 1971), *Family and Social Networks*, London, Tavistock.

BRIGGS, A., and OLIVER, J. (eds.) (1985), *Caring: Experiences of Looking After Disabled Relatives*, London, Routledge and Kegan Paul.

BULMER, M. (1986), *Neighbours: The Work of Philip Abrams*, Cambridge, Cambridge University Press.

CANCIAN, F. (1987), *Love in America: Gender and Social Development*, Cambridge, Cambridge University Press.

COHEN, T. (1992), 'Men's families, men's friendships: a structural analysis of constraints on men's social ties', in Nardi (ed.) (1992).

COTTERILL, P. (1994), *Friendly Relations: Mothers and their Daughters-in-Law*, London, Taylor and Francis.

CROW, G., and ALLAN, G. (1990), 'Constructing the domestic sphere: the emergence of the modern home in post-war Britain', in Corr, H., and Jamieson, L. (eds.), *Politics of Everyday Life: Continuity and Change in Work and the Family*, London, Macmillan.

—————— (1994), *Community Life: An Introduction to Local Social Relationships*, Hemel Hempstead, Harvester Wheatsheaf.

CUNNINGHAM-BURLEY, S. (1985), 'Constructing grandparenthood: anticipating appropriate action', *Sociology*, 19: 421–36.

DEEM, R. (1982), 'Women, leisure and inequality', *Leisure Studies*, 1: 229–46.

DENNIS, N., HENRIQUES, F., and SLAUGHTER, C. (1956), *Coal is our Life: An Analysis of a Yorkshire Mining Community*, London, Tavistock.

DEVINE, F. (1992), *Affluent Workers Revisited: Privatism and the Working Class*, Edinburgh, Edinburgh University Press.

DICKENS, W. J., and PERLMAN, D. (1981), 'Friendship over the Life Cycle', in Duck, S. W., and Gilmour, R. (eds.), *Personal Relationships: 2. Developing Personal Relationships*, New York, Academic Press.

DI LEONARDO, M. (1987), 'The female world of cards and holidays: women, families and the work of kinship', *Signs*, 12: 440–58.

DUCK, S. (1990), 'Relationships as unfinished business: out of the frying pan and into the 1990s', *Journal of Social and Personal Relationships*, 7: 5–28.

EDGELL, S. (1980), *Middle Class Couples*, London, Allen and Unwin.

FINCH, J. (1987), 'The vignette technique in survey research', *Sociology*, 21: 105–14.

—— (1989), *Family Obligations and Social Change*, Cambridge, Polity Press.

—— and GROVES, D. (eds.) (1983), *A Labour of Love*, London, Routledge and Kegan Paul.

—— and MASON, J. (1990), 'Divorce, remarriage and family obligations', *Sociological Review*, 38: 219–46.

—— —— (1993), *Negotiating Family Responsibilities*, London, Routledge.

FIRTH, R. (1956), *Two Studies of Kinship in London*, London, Athlone.

—— HUBERT, J., and FORGE, A. (1970), *Families and their Relatives*, London, Routledge and Kegan Paul.

FISCHER, C., and OLIKER, S. (1983), 'A research note on friendship, gender and the life cycle', *Social Forces*, 62: 124–33.

FORREST, R., MURIE, A., and WILLIAMS, P. (1990), *Home Ownership: Differentiation and Fragmentation*, London, Unwin Hyman.

FRANKENBERG, R. (1957), *Village on the Border: A Social Study of Religion, Politics and Football in a North Wales Community*, London, Cohen and West.

FRANKLIN, A. (1989), 'Working class privatism: an historical case study of Bedminster, Bristol', *Environment and Planning D: Society and Space*, 7: 93–113.

GALLIE, D., GERSHUNY, J., and VOGLER, C. (1994), 'Unemployment, the household, and social networks', in Gallie *et al.* (1994).

—— MARSH, C., and VOGLER, C. (eds.) (1994), *Social Change and the Experience of Unemployment*, Oxford, Oxford University Press.

GANS, H. (1962), *The Urban Villagers*, New York, Free Press.

GIDDENS, A. (1991), *Modernity and Self-Identity*, Cambridge, Polity.

—— (1992), *The Transformation of Intimacy*, Cambridge, Polity.

GITTINS, D. (1993), *The Family in Question*, London, Macmillan.

GOFFMAN, E. (1959), *The Presentation of Self in Everyday Life*, Garden City, NY, Doubleday Anchor.

GOLDTHORPE, J. H., LOCKWOOD, D., BECHHOFER, F., and PLATT, J. (1969), *The Affluent Worker in the Class Structure*, Cambridge, Cambridge University Press.

GRIECO, M. (1987), *Keeping it in the Family: Social Networks and Employment Chance*, London, Tavistock.

HARRIS, C. C. (1969), *The Family: An Introduction*, London, Allen and Unwin.

—— (1990), *Kinship*, Milton Keynes, Open University Press.

HART, N. (1976), *When Marriage Ends*, London, Tavistock.

HESS, B. (1972), 'Friendship', in Riley, M. W., Johnson, M., and Foner, A. (eds.), *Aging and Society. Vol. 3: A Sociology of Age Stratification*, New York, Russell Sage.

—— (1979), 'Sex roles, friendship and the life course', *Research on Aging*, 1: 494–515.

HOBSON, D. (1978), 'Housewives: isolation as oppression', in Women's Study Group, Centre for Contemporary Cultural Studies, *Women Take Issue*, London, Hutchinson.

HUNT, G., and SATTERLEE, S. (1986), 'Cohesion and division: drinking in an English

References

village', *Man*, 21: 521–37.

——— (1987), 'Darts, drinks and the pub: the culture of female drinking', *Sociological Review*, 35: 575–601.

Hutson, S., and Jenkins, R. (1989), *Taking the Strain: Families, Unemployment and the Transition to Adulthood*, Milton Keynes, Open University Press.

Jerrome, D. (1981), 'The significance of friendship for women in later life', *Ageing and Society*, 1: 175–97.

——— (1984), 'Good company: the sociological implications of friendship', *Sociological Review*, 32: 696–718.

——— (1992), *Good Company: An Anthropological Study of Old People in Groups*, Edinburgh, Edinburgh University Press.

Jones, G. (1995), *Leaving Home*, Milton Keynes, Open University Press.

Leonard, D. (1980), *Sex and Generation: A Study of Courtship and Weddings*, London, Tavistock.

Lewis, J., and Meredith, B. (1988), *Daughters Who Care: Daughters Caring for Mothers at Home*, London, Routledge.

Litwak, E. (1985), *Helping the Elderly: The Complementary Roles of Informal Networks and Formal Systems*, New York, Guilford.

——— (1989), 'Forms of friendships among older people in an industrial society', in Adams and Blieszner (eds.) (1989).

Lund, M. (1987), 'The non-custodial father: common challenges in parenting after divorce', in Lewis, C., and O'Brien, M. (eds.), *Reassessing Fatherhood: New Observations on Fathers and the Modern Family*, London, Sage.

Lupton, T., and Wilson, C. S. (1959), 'The social background and connections of "top decision-makers"', *The Manchester School*, 27: 30–51.

McKee, L. (1987), 'Households during unemployment: the resourcefulness of the unemployed', in Brannen, J., and Wilson, G. (eds.), *Give and Take in Families: Studies in Resource Distribution*, London, Allen and Unwin.

——— and Bell, C. (1986), 'His unemployment, her problem: the domestic and marital consequences of male unemployment', in Allen, S., Waton, A., Purcell, K., and Wood, S. (eds.), *The Experience of Unemployment*, London, Macmillan.

Mansfield, P., and Collard, J. (1987), *The Beginning of the Rest of Your Life? A Portrait of Newly-Wed Marriage*, London, Macmillan.

Marks, S. (1994), 'Intimacy in the public realm: the case of co-workers', *Social Forces*, 72: 843–58.

Mason, D. (1995), *Race and Ethnicity in Modern Britain*, Oxford, Oxford University Press.

Milardo, R. (1987), 'Changes in social networks of women and men following divorce: a review', *Journal of Family Issues*, 8: 78–96.

——— (1992), 'Comparative methods for delineating social networks', *Journal of Social and Personal Relationships*, 9: 447–61.

——— and Allan, G. (1996), 'Social networks and marital relationships', in Duck, S., Dindia, K., Milardo, R., Mills, R., and Sarason, B. (eds.), *Handbook of Personal Relationships*, London, Wiley.

Mitchell, J. C. (1974), 'Social Networks', *Annual Review of Anthropology*, 3: 279–

99.

MOGEY, J. (1956), *Family and Neighbourhood*, London, Oxford University Press.

MORGAN, D. (1975), *Social Theory and the Family*, London, Routledge and Kegan Paul.

MORRIS, L. (1990), *The Workings of the Household*, Cambridge, Polity.

NARDI, P. (ed.) (1992), *Men's Friendships*, Newbury Park, Sage.

NISSEL, M., and BONNERJEA, L. (1982), *Family Care for the Handicapped Elderly: Who Pays?*, London, Policy Studies Institute.

OAKLEY, A. (1974), *The Sociology of Housework*, London, Martin Robertson.

O'BRIEN, M. (1987), 'Patterns of kinship and friendship among lone fathers', in Lewis, C., and O'Brien, M. (eds.), *Reassessing Fatherhood: New Observations on Fathers and the Modern Family*, London, Sage.

O'CONNOR, P. (1990), 'The adult mother-daughter relationship: a uniquely and universally close relationship?', *Sociological Review*, 38: 293–323.

—— (1992), *Friendships between Women*, Hemel Hempstead, Harvester Wheatsheaf.

OLIKER, S. (1989), *Best Friends and Marriage: Exchange among Women*, Berkeley, Calif., University of California Press.

OXLEY, H. G. (1974), *Mateship in Local Organization*, Queensland, University of Queensland Press.

PAHL, R. E. (1965), *Urbs in Rure: The Metropolitan Fringe in Hertfordshire*, Papers in Geography, No. 2, London, London School of Economics.

—— (1984), *Divisions of Labour*, Oxford, Blackwell.

—— and WALLACE, C. D. (1988), 'Neither angels in marble nor rebels in red: privatization and working-class consciousness', in Rose, D. (ed.), *Social Stratification and Economic Change*, London, Hutchinson.

PARKER, R. (1981), 'Tending and social policy', in Goldberg, E. M., and Hatch, S. (eds.), *A New Look at the Personal Social Services*, London, Policy Studies Institute.

PARSONS, T. (1943), 'The kinship system of the contemporary United States', *American Anthropologist*, 45: 22–38.

—— (1956), 'The American family: its relations to personality and to the social structure', in Parsons, T., and Bales, R. (eds.), *Family: Socialisation and Interaction Process*, London, Routledge and Kegan Paul.

PERISTIANY, J. (1976), *Mediterranean Family Structures*, Cambridge, Cambridge University Press.

PLECK, J. H. (1976), 'Man to man: is brotherhood possible?', in Glazer-Malbin, N. (ed.), *Old Family/New Family: Interpersonal Relationships*, New York, Van Nostrand.

POOL, I., and KOCHEN, M. (1978), 'Contacts and influence', *Social Networks*, 1: 5–51.

PROCTER, I. (1990), 'The privatisation of working-class life', *British Journal of Sociology*, 41: 157–80.

QURESHI, H., and WALKER, A. (1989), *The Caring Relationship: Elderly People and their Families*, London, Macmillan.

REES, A. D. (1950), *Life in a Welsh Countryside*, Cardiff, University of Wales Press.

References

REID, H., and FINE, G. (1992), 'Self-disclosure in men's friendships: variations associated with intimate relations', in Nardi (ed.) (1992).

ROBINSON, M., and SMITH, D. (1993), *Step by Step: Focus on Stepfamilies*, Hemel Hempstead, Harvester Wheatsheaf.

ROSENTHAL, C. (1985), 'Kinkeeping in the familial division of labor', *Journal of Marriage and the Family*, 47: 965–74.

ROSSER, C., and HARRIS, C. C. (1965, 1983), *The Family and Social Change: A Study of Family and Kinship in a South Wales Town*, London, Routledge and Kegan Paul.

RUBIN, L. B. (1985), *Just Friends: The Role of Friendship in Our Lives*, New York, Harper and Row.

SAUNDERS, P. (1990), *A Nation of Home Owners*, London, Unwin Hyman.

SCHNEIDER, D. (1968), *American Kinship: A Cultural Account*, Englewood Cliffs, NJ, Prentice-Hall.

SCOTT, J. (1991), *Social Network Analysis: A Handbook*, London, Sage.

ST LEGER, F., and GILLESPIE, N. (1991), *Informal Welfare in Belfast: Caring Communities?*, Aldershot, Avebury.

STRATHERN, M. (1981), *Kinship at the Core: An Anthropology of Elmdon, a Village in North-West Essex in the Nineteen-Sixties*, Cambridge, Cambridge University Press.

SUITOR, J. (1987), 'Friendship networks in transitions: married mothers' return to school', *Journal of Social and Personal Relationships*, 4: 445–61.

TIGER, L. (1969), *Men in Groups*, New York, Random House.

TÖNNIES, F. (1955), *Community and Association*, London, Routledge and Kegan Paul.

TOWNSEND, P. (1963), *The Family Life of Old People*, Harmondsworth, Penguin.

UNGERSON, C. (1987), *Policy is Personal: Sex, Gender and Informal Care*, London, Tavistock.

WALLACE, C. (1987), *For Richer, For Poorer: Growing Up In and Out of Work*, London, Tavistock.

WARRIER, S. (1994), 'Gujarati Prajapatis in London: family roles and sociability networks', in Ballard (ed.) (1994).

WELLMAN, B. (1979), 'The community question', *American Journal of Sociology*, 84: 1201–31.

—— (1985), 'Domestic work, paid work and net work', in Duck, S., and Perlman, D. (eds.), *Understanding Personal Relationships*, London, Sage.

—— (1988), 'Structural analysis: from method and metaphor to theory and substance', in Wellman and Berkowitz (eds.) (1988).

—— (1992), 'Men in networks: private communities, domestic friendships', in Nardi (ed.) (1992).

—— and BERKOWITZ, S. D. (eds.) (1988), *Social Structures: A Network Approach*, Cambridge, Cambridge University Press.

—— and WORTLEY, S. (1990), 'Different strokes from different folks: community ties and social support', *American Journal of Sociology*, 96: 558–88.

—— CARRINGTON, P. J., and HALL, A. (1988), 'Networks as personal communities', in Wellman and Berkowitz (eds.) (1988).

WENGER, G. C. (1984), *The Supportive Network*, London, Allen and Unwin.

—— (1989), 'Support networks in old age—constructing a typology', in Jefferys, M. (ed.), *Growing Old in the Twentieth Century*, London, Routledge.

—— (1995), 'A comparison of urban with rural support networks: Liverpool and North Wales', *Ageing and Society*, 15: 59–81.

WERBNER, P. (1981), 'Manchester Pakistanis: lifestyles, ritual and the making of social distinctions', *New Community*, 9: 216–28.

WESTWOOD, S., and BHACHU, P. (1988), *Enterprising Women: Ethnicity, Economy and Gender Relations*, London, Routledge.

WILLIAMS, R. G. A. (1983), 'Kinship and migration strategies among settled Londoners: two responses to population pressure', *British Journal of Sociology*, 34: 386–415.

WILLIAMS, W. M. (1956), *The Sociology of an English Village: Gosforth*, London, Routledge and Kegan Paul.

—— (1963), *A West Country Village: Ashworthy*, London, Routledge and Kegan Paul.

WILLMOTT, P. (1963), *The Evolution of a Community*, London, Routledge and Kegan Paul.

—— (1986), *Social Networks, Informal Care and Public Policy*, London, Policy Studies Institute.

—— (1987), *Friendship Networks and Social Support*, London, Policy Studies Institute.

—— and YOUNG, M. (1960), *Family and Class in a London Suburb*, London, Routledge and Kegan Paul.

WILSON, P., and PAHL, R. E. (1988), 'The changing sociological construct of the family', *Sociological Review*, 36: 223–66.

WIRTH, L. (1938), 'Urbanism as a way of life', *American Journal of Sociology*, 44: 1–24.

WRIGHT, P. (1982), 'Men's friendships, women's friendships and the alleged inferiority of the latter', *Sex Roles*, 8: 1–20.

YOUNG, M., and WILLMOTT, P. (1957), *Family and Kinship in East London*, London, Routledge and Kegan Paul.

Index

Index

domestic:
  division of labour 11
  life-style 14
  responsibilities 103
Donald 42, 43, 49
drinking patterns 104
Duck, S. 2

East York 123
Edgell, S. 11
effective kin 32
Eid 41
Eire 28
elderly people, numbers of 67–8
employment 78
  married women's 46
engagement 34, 57
equality in friendship 89
ethnic minorities, second generation 50
exchange in friendship 89–90
extended family 8

family:
  commitments 78–9
  and kinship 26–7
  reputation 45
  responsibility 56
female sociability 17
femininity 94, 113
Finch, J. 4, 35, 44, 47, 51, 66, 70, 72, 73, 74,
  75, 76, 77, 78, 79, 80, 82, 83
Fine, G. 93
Firth, R. 27, 30, 31, 32, 35, 37, 39, 40, 42,
  43, 44, 51, 52, 54, 121
Fischer, C. 94
Forge, A. 30, 31, 35
formal roles 111–13
Forrest, R. 15
Frankenberg, R. 28
Franklin, A. 19, 88, 129
friends, best 90
  using 108
friendship and cultural scripts 99
  defining 84–5
  and divorce 96
  the ending of 95
  face-to-face 93–4
  formation 87
  and inequality 91–2
  and the life course 95–6
  and promotion 97

  as a resource 108–9
  resources 93
  side-by-side 93
  and social position 91, 95, 100–1
  studies 84

Gallie, D. 62, 108
Gans, H. 8
gender and caring 71, 72–3
  identity 92
  and parent–child ties 59–60
genealogies 30, 31
General Household Survey 68
generating social networks 118–20
geographical:
  distance 79
  mobility 95, 97, 105
Giddens, A. 6, 12, 116
gift-giving 34, 61–2, 81
Gilbert, N. 72
Gillespie, N. 83
Ginn, J. 69
Gittins, D. 21
Glynceiriog 28
Goffman, E. 63
Goldthorpe, J. H. 9, 21
Gosforth 28
gossip 41, 94
granny flat 81
Grieco, M. 35, 42
Groves, D. 72, 73

Harris, C. C. 8, 30, 32, 33, 34, 35, 36, 42, 46,
  49, 53, 59, 60
Hart, N. 47, 96
Hawthorne experiments 2
Hess, B. 93, 101, 111
Hobson, D. 108
home 104
  entertaining 18, 87, 88
  furnishings 16
  ownership 15–16
  as self-expression 16
households 72
housing standards 14
Hubert, J. 30, 31, 35
Hunt, G. 103
Hutson, S. 57

ideology of marriage 11–12
immediate social environment 100–1, 104,
  106, 113

Index

Townsend, P. 29, 32, 35
traditional working class communities 15, 29, 59

unemployment 62, 108
Ungerson, C. 63, 72, 79
United States 3, 84
unmarried mothers 47
urban community studies 29
urbanism 7

vignettes 74–5
Vogler, C. 62

Wales 28, 125
Walker, A. 35, 70, 73, 74, 82, 83
Wallace, C. 17, 57
Warrier, S. 49, 50
wealth-holding 80

Wellman, B. 17, 20, 100, 101, 107, 108, 118, 123, 124, 125, 129, 130
Wenger, C. 125, 126
Werbner, P. 50, 51
Westwood, S. 49
widowhood 96, 105
Williams, R. 95
Williams, W. M. 28
Willmott, P. 8, 15, 18, 29, 32, 35, 36, 98, 108
Wilson, C. 36
Wilson, P. 4
Wirth, L. 7
workplace studies 2
Wortley, S. 20, 123, 125
Wright, P. 93

Yeandle, S. 57
Young, M. 8, 15, 29, 32, 35, 36